FACILITATING ORGANIZATIONAL CHANGE

Daniel A. Silverman

University Press of America, Inc.
Lanham • New York • London

Copyright © 1996 by
University Press of America,® Inc.
4720 Boston Way
Lanham, Maryland 20706

3 Henrietta Street
London, WC2E 8LU England

Library of Congress Cataloging-in-Publication Data

Silverman, Daniel A.
Facilitating organizational change / Daniel A. Silverman.
p.   cm.
Includes bibliographical references and index.
l. Organizational change. I. Title.
HD58/8S574   1996   658.4'06 --dc20   96-34220 CIP

ISBN 0-7618-0491-9 (cloth: alk. ppr.)
ISBN 0-7618-0492-7 (pbk: alk. ppr.)

Quotes from the work of Edward T. Hall originally appeared in The Silent Language, Garden City, NY:
Doubleday, 1959. Quoted by permission of Dr. Edward T. Hall.

∞™ The paper used in this publication meets the minimum
requirements of American National Standard for information
Sciences—Permanence of Paper for Printed Library Materials,
ANSI Z39.48—1984

Table of Contents

Author's Preface

This work is being written as a foundation piece for assisting others to look at cultural change from multi-faceted perspectives. The beauty of using various lenses to view culture is that with each lens you see something different. When you put all the different perspectives together it is possible to see a design that previously was impossible to see.

Few would question the fact that cultural analysis and cultural change are the two most difficult things individuals can do. Extensive research by researcher Edward T. Hall has revealed pretty conclusively that it is almost impossible to understand the lines of force in our culture. He believes that the best that the analysis of cultures different from ours can give is a rough insight into how different the two cultures are.

In light of the above, we have to admit freely that when we intervene into a cultural environment as facilitators of change, we get hit with a double whammy--the new culture is similar enough to ours that we are prevented from seeing the complexity of the lines of forces within it and it so much is the culture of another group that it is hard for us to get close enough to intervene into it in a meaningful way. It is hoped that this book will assist all of us in building these multi-faceted perspectives so that we can truly facilitate change in a way that does not cause our expulsion from the culture.

The most influential teacher in my life, anthropologist Edward T. Hall, told me that writing was like taking a pound of flesh from the middle of his back. That, indeed, has been the case for most of my writing; this book is an exception. This book is being written from my heart and head in the hopes that it might help eliminate some of the headache out there which evolves from organizational change efforts.

Throughout this work, I will be referring to situations that I have experienced during my past twenty years of cultural change work. I have worked very hard to disguise specific clients and situations, and at the same time to retain most of the flavor of the events. I believe I have been successful.

Included within these pages, are the learnings that I have accumulated over the past twenty years. Some of them came because of my brilliant insights; some came because I have made some occasionally really stupid, albeit really well meaning, mistakes. Regardless of how the knowledge was amassed, generalizations and maps of terrain that the reader will encounter out there have come from the clients with whom I have been blessed. They include:

A.T.&T.
Colegio Cristobal Colon
Carnegie Mellon University
Chubb Insurance Companies
Fannie Mae
Ford Motor Company
General Electric
General Motors
James River Corporation
PSE&G
U.S. Department of Agriculture
U.S. Department of Commerce
U.S. Department of the Navy
U.S. Department of the Treasury
U.S. Immigration and Naturalization Service
U.S. Postal Service
University of California, Santa Cruz
University of Pennsylvania

My clients represent a broad spectrum of enterprise types and, I feel, in the composite can serve as the foundation for the development of generalizable models. I wish to thank each of them for the opportunity of working with, and, most importantly, learning from them.

I wish to acknowledge those unique individuals who have driven me to learn more about how change works--Ed Hall,

Lee Roloff, Matt and Carolina. I would like to pay special tribute to the greatest teacher of them all, Maria Clemencia, who introduced me to Latin American culture and who is constantly reintroducing me to my own. Thank you.

Introduction

"If God took seven days to create the earth and the planets, it would take him significantly longer to make even a small dent in the way in which any one of the federal bureaucracies works; He might want to avoid some departments completely." An Unidentified Bureaucrat

"It was becoming more and more clear to me that the things I wanted to understand, that I was curious about, that would please me if I found out about them--equilibrium wasn't an important part of any of them."

John Holland, The Santa Fe Institute

When facilitators enter into a change situation, they are setting into action a profoundly complex set of actions and reactions that must first be understood and then managed. The difficulty rests with the difficulty of their understanding of what they are dealing with during the transformational process. They look with a mind conditioned by their past experiences. They feel disoriented and confused.

Rather than using the state of disequilibrium created at the time of cultural entry as one in which they can explore and discover, there is both an external push from their management and an internal push by their egos to return to a state of equilibrium without exploring the complexity which faces them. Each time any of us looks at a change intervention, we, in reality, are standing at the edge overlooking the abyss. It is important that each of us recognize the danger and prepare ourselves by designing ways of mitigating risk.

The all encompassing reason for this danger is that the investigator assumes that the models that they have developed during their lifetimes for "reality" are generalizable to others. Change facilitators believe that what they learned working for the Department of Commerce is generalizable to the U.S. Postal Service; they believe that what they learned at General Electric is transferable to General Motors. They believe that what they might have done for their MBA work somehow prepared them for intervening into a milieu with which they are completely unfamiliar. Their assumptions which I have shared also are almost always wrong.

Each of us carries around in our head a design of how we think the universe should be. A universe that is described in a series of tapes that run below our levels of consciousness and which very few of us acknowledge are there, let alone understand.

The role of the external consultant is to intervene into the cultural milieu, to reflect back to its members what they see, and to provide visibility for the options that the members have available to them for transforming their culture. Clearly, such a task is monumental. The change management facilitator is asked to assist in transforming an organization against the power brokers who are firmly entrenched in the culture; the consultant is to do this from a position of weakness--a formidable lack of a power base--in a culture foreign to them.

Culture hides environments from us. It programs us into filtering out what it does not want us to see. It lulls us into believing that such screening processes not only allow us to see the truth, but that other options for viewing things are really not viable.

Benjamin Lee Whorf, Edward Sapir, T.S. Kuhn, Edward T. Hall, and a long line of other scholars, have arrived at the same conclusion--essentially, we are prisoners of the screens that our culture inculcates in us. We become what we are programmed to see. We see only our pasts when we look to the future. Though such structures are valuable in maintaining and perpetuating specific components of our cultures, they make it very difficult for us to adapt in substantive ways to the demands placed upon us by threatening external phenomena.

Change agents are being asked to intervene in cultures that, in addition to being relatively incomprehensible to those within them, and foreign to those from without, are being forced through the crucible of unheralded competition. Manufacturing industries in the United States continue to shrink as foreign competition attracts dollars for their products. There are daily news notices of both service and manufacturing company downsizings. U.S. firms create strategic alliances with international partners, and their competitors, to reduce product R&D cycle time. American products are outsourced to foreign companies for manufacturing at reduced labor rates.

The globalization of economies and the resultant interdependencies cause massive pressures to build in the U.S. How does a light bulb manufacturing plant in Illinois compete with one in Korea with a 5:1 labor cost differential? How does the Detroit automobile manufacturer compete with a maquiladora plant with 6:1 labor cost ratios? What impact does international competition have upon our organizational cultures and the need for them to provide the roadmaps for dealing with this outrageous change? Even in government, agencies are fighting one another for scarcer resources and now the electorate questions whether they are getting an appropriate return on their investment.

At a more human level, what happens to individuals who are moved from one work environment to another. I once had to intervene into the horror of coping with the frustration of a group of Amish farmers who lost their land and had to come and work on a cabinet manufacturing line; they went from a physical rootedness to the land, under the sun, breathing fresh air to an environment filled with sawdust, polyurethane, and disorientation. Research suggests that moving almost anyone from work that is contexted to that which is not causes very fundamental shifts in the ways folks relate to their environments and what their emotion state is like within them.

Called to the forefront of this massive change are Change Management consultants who are being accessed for leadership through these uncertain times. How can our culture, which gravitates towards inertia, be used to move us towards identifying, accepting, leveraging, and perpetuating continuous change as a vehicle for increasing our standards of living? They know that they and their clients are at the cusp of change, but that most models from the past are of little utility. The conundrum is that as the investigators of what high potential territories lie beyond the horizon, they, as their clients, can well become prisoners of their cultural assumptions relative to what their roles as change agents are and should be. The cultural rules which constitute the screening options available to members of the change management community can allow it to succumb to the drive towards inertia which all other cultural entities are susceptible.

In this book, we will explore the various lenses that will allow us to look at change milieus from multiple perspectives.

In Chapter 1, we will establish a framework for looking at change from multi-faceted perspectives. This framework will serve as the basis for all other content in the book.

In Chapter 2, we will explore the building of a psychological model with which we can approach a new environment. Our objective is not to make the facilitators over into psychologists, but to create a conceptual framework by which they can map kinds of behaviors and understand the drives and motivations of their clients. In addition, techniques will be provided to map critical behaviors that are necessary for the engagement to be a success.

In Chapter 3, we will investigate building a personal model of how culture works and provide an initial set of tools and techniques for building models with the cultures of readers' clients.

In Chapter 4, we will explore the infrastructural components present in the intervention and how we can use these as levers for cultural change.

Chapter5 is the summary of this work.

Appendix A covers the Hall Trager System for the analysis of culture.

Chapter 1

Change and Building A Framework to Facilitate It

The Moffat Tunnel runs for seven miles under the Continental Divide in Western Colorado. Its sole purpose is to allow trains to bypass any of the gigantic mountains that lurk overhead; they cut right through them. On its east side is a parking lot where people come to look at some giant fans kick in and blow all the diesel smoke out the west end. Of course, they cannot see it, but they happily fantasize as they look at the thick rubber curtain as it is pressurized during the extraction process.

Between extractions, railroad people are required to go into the dark hole to accomplish whatever they need to accomplish. It is awesomely quiet there. There are only the occasional scamperings of mice who are out of their shelters feeding on the various grains that have fallen from the freight cars. There are no rats here; worker legend has it that the lack of rats suggests that there is either a gas leak or the place is ready to cave in. The workers swear that the rats are more intelligent than we are.

Five hundred yards into the tunnel from either end, you cannot see light. It is totally dark. Four miles in and you forget what seeing was like. Even the light on top of your hard-hat is swallowed up by the diesel smoke shroud that covers everything. Everything is diesel black; it's like a sponge.

Every quarter mile there are cave-in shelters. They consist of nothing more that a concrete cube one foot thick on all sides with a telephone in it. The door is thick also and creaks when you open it.

The workers have to open the doors twice a month to make sure that they are not rusted shut, that the phone lines have not been eaten through by the mice, and, most important, shovel the mice out. In one month those promiscuous critters get to be three feet deep. They have to be shoveled out because no one would want to touch them. When the helmet lights hit their orbs that have adapted to darkness, they go crazy. They scurry up and down the worker's pants, squeaking in fright, and panicked by the fact that such a great standard of living had such an abrupt end.

Contrary to commonly held intuition regarding cultural change, all of us tend to behave as the mice do. We too run around hysterically looking for a way of re-engaging the old. It is not that we are not bright and talented people and, therefore, act like mice. It is that we are first and foremost biological entities and that no matter how much culture we immerse ourselves in, when change comes it hits us the same as it does the rest of the animal world and our reaction is unbelievably similar.

Throughout this work, it will be argued that the very nature of culture is to maintain the status quo and to use all means available to it to communicate the need for stability. The Pope as a maintainer of the Catholic Church's culture has ruled that women cannot become priests--a ruling that has caused consternation among his followers that he is out of touch with the times. Rather than accept the desires of members of the culture and adapt the culture of the Church to them, the Pope threatens excommunication to any woman who says Mass or any Catholic who attends it. The position is that if anyone wants to change that culture along a few critical lines, they are expelled from the culture.

Parents often times establish unbreakable rules that take on a life of their own regardless of the fact that circumstances for the rules have changed. For instance, they rule when their daughter is a sophomore in high school that she needs to be in by 11:30 p.m.. Their daughter is very compliant with their rule all during high school. However, when she comes for holiday break during her Freshman Year in college, where she has established her own schedules and rules, she becomes incredulous that the parents think that they have the right to enforce such childish rules. If there is a discussion regarding this between her and her parents, it becomes pretty clear that rationality is not the main mode operating here and that we have a new culture of the daughter's that models how she behaves.

Historically, cultures have been safe relatively from change from within. All sorts of mechanisms including the courts, the police, religious entities, social and country clubs, parent teacher organizations, the military, the upper classes, individuals who bore prestigious names, governments, and others were available to stop threats from within. The bad news is that these same internal entities are now hiring change interventionists who are sanctioned usually by only one component of the culture to help transform it. Paradoxically, our clients bring us in to change the culture because they have not been able to do it themselves and they know that it cannot be done, but they commit significant funds to it nevertheless. Those who are interested in supporting our facilitation of true change are visionaries of their own domains assigning their strong faith in organizational transformation to our skill and intelligence.

Unfortunately most interventions do not nudge an organization to sustainable cultural change. Most will result in recommendations being made that affect personnel, organizational structure, fundamental ways of going about the business and configuring the processes; almost none of these are pushed to the point where they touch upon organizational change. That is not to suggest that intelligence and skills are not applied by the consultants. It does suggest that our interventionists face very serious obstacles and that the organizational change toolboxes that they carry into the situation are not suited optimally for the work that needs to be done.

The essence of effective intervention in organizations is the ability to lead individuals within that organization into a new way of interacting with each other and, even more profoundly, into looking at the world in a different way. It is a serious mistake to assume that individuals will embrace change when they have not been deprogrammed from seeing the world in the old way. They need to be weaned from systems that constitute their old beliefs and need to be given viable, meaningful alternatives so that they will have an orientation in the new world.

The single greatest differentiator between those successful organizational change consultants and the much larger number of truly hard working but unsuccessful facilitators out there is the sophistication of the cultural conceptual toolbox that they assemble and maintain. Though the toolboxes appear relatively simple, the tools are very complex and a broad array of these tools is required to work effectively in any environment undergoing transformation. The whole point of the toolbox is to force the facilitator into looking at the change phenomena as robustly as possible and forcing them to approach it from a multitude of perspectives.

Components of Organizational Change

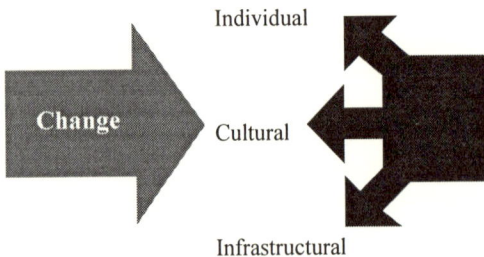

Individual

Change → Cultural

Infrastructural

At its highest level, Organizational Change has to be approached using three classes of models, all of which will be used to smoke out patterns occurring within the milieu.

Individual Models will be used to identify specific psychological characteristics, personality types within the client organization, and the psychological levers that can be used effectively to modify dysfunctional client behaviors. For instance, it is becoming more and more common for no one at the client site to take on the roles of leadership during consulting engagements; there is a sense that everyone is *Waiting for Godot* and that complaining about nothing happening somehow remedies the problem.

Cultural Models are used to track in a scientific way exactly what Primary Message System or Systems are being attacked by the consultant intervention. Anthropologists have developed sophisticated systems for tracking change. Culture is defined as communication and communication is culture; models provided by Hall, Trager, and the author provide tools for developing communication plans   once communication needs have been assessed.

Infrastructural Models are used to assess current reinforcers of behaviors and to modify them for developing alternative systems. For instance, executives all too often feel that they want to radically change their organizations to empower people but they are a bit reticent about acknowledging that such empowerment cannot change the hierarchical, pay for individual initiative-only behaviors that are a critical part of their culture.

Further break out of components under each of the categories will follow during the next three chapters; undoubtedly the reader has some of the slots filled. The key point is to be able to use a minimum of five tools at a client site at any given time to detect the lines of force occurring within that environment. Below are models that have proven highly successful in the field; the more complex the models held by the facilitator, the higher the chances of success.

Once facilitators define each of the models below for themselves, elaborate upon their frameworks, and become comfortable with them, it is time to determine how to best use the tools.

Components of Organizational Change

Individual	Cultural	Infrastructural
Massey Generational	1. Interaction	1. Skill Decomposition
Ornstein Spherical	2. Association	2. Behavioral Maps
Freudian Depth	3. Subsistence	3. Job Definition
Ellis Rational/Emotive	4.Genetic Promulgation	4. Comp Structures
Rogerian Self-Affirm.	5. Territoriality	5. Org. Acculturation
	6. Temporality	6. Recruitment
	7. Learning	7. Career Progression
	8. Play	8. Development
	9. Defense	9. Feedback Mechs
	10. Exploitation	10. Non-Comp Drivers

The Models

As in other fields of study, to be successful in the realm of psycho-cultural intervention, one needs to be able to differentiate between a wide array of cultures, individuals, and their behaviors. As in other fields, the use of models serves the purpose of giving the researcher and interventionist tools by which they can examine the various psycho-cultural components and identify the patterns of behavior that can serve as the basis for their intervention.

The various models provided are not exhaustive. Criteria for their selection are that they have been shown to be successful by anthropologists, psychologists, and consultants in the field. In the next chapter, we will focus primarily upon the individual level. We will utilize several cultural models for analysis in the following chapter, and we will examine infrastructural models used and developed by the author in the chapter following that. Each interventionist should choose a set of tools for his/her toolbox, as well as be open to the possibility that they will have to create hybrid tools or invent brand new tools to optimize the chances of their success across a wide range of environmental mixes.

Chapter 2

Models of the Individual

Overview

An individual clearly is a part of the culture that has raised and nourished him/her. It is an inescapable fact that we many times catch ourselves reacting to a new situation with the emotional patterns of those with whom we live. Much as we hate to admit it, we have been programmed to react by the codes generated within us by others and it is a monumental undertaking to erase that code forever. I react in some ways as my father did, and he reacted in the same way that his father-- my grandfather reacted, and my grandfather reacted in the same way that my great grandfather reacted. To any careful observer, cross-generational ghosts hide within the living only to present themselves at the least expected moments.

Peter Drucker identified our dependency upon what we have learned from our earlier environment. He believes that we fundamentally are trapped by what we learned from the environment of our formative years and that it is very difficult to grow out of it. He believes that if we are to be judged an adult that by the age of thirty-five we need to take responsibility for our own face--we no longer can blame others for what looks back at us from the bathroom mirror in the morning. The fact is that we can never escape our culture's impact upon us. It never will allow us to escape.

However, though the individual is the repository of culture, he/she can absorb highly idiosyncratic components of that culture to the exclusion of that which is mainstream, or that individual may be so idiosyncratic that very little cultural imprint can be detected in them. It is difficult for us to identify examples that all of us share, but certain icons do come to mind. Luciano Pavarotti and Sophia Loren are embodiments of their environment--Italy--but they also stand out from it with their own eccentricities and lifestyles. Picasso was always culturally Spanish but he embodied the idiosyncrasies of the Bohemian artist viewing the world transcendent of his Spanish origins. Gabriel Garcia Marquez is the embodiment of Colombia's coastal culture, but his position as an outsider creates a unique story in *One Hundred Years of Solitude* that describes us all.

The purpose of this chapter is to focus upon the individual dimensions of people that separate them one from the other within the all encompassing embrace of the total culture. For our purposes, we will restrict ourselves to individuals who do not demonstrate aberrant behaviors or mental illness pathologies.

Experience had demonstrated that by looking at phenomena from various vantage points we can see a picture that is more descriptive of a whole. We will utilize Massey's Generational Model, the Spherical Function Model, the Tapes/Stories Model, components of Freud's Psychoanalytical Model, and Ellis' Rational Emotive Psychoanalytical Model. Our job is to identify those models that can serve as constructs for digging out the differences.

1. The Generational Model

Maurice Massey first identified that four generational models are of value in defining broad classes of people; he believed that individuals were defined relative to their value sets impressed upon them depending upon where they were when. He maintains that there are certain formative events that significantly affect the ways that people are.

Though Massey's theory errs on the side of simplicity, it does allow for a relatively rapid analysis of organizational characteristics. When his models are used in conjunction with other tools, significant insights can accrue.

Following Massey's theories, two events had a very profound effect upon the way in which individuals of my generation see the world. John F. Kennedy was assassinated when I was in 9th Grade; Dr. King was assassinated when I was a freshman in college. Both events, when coupled with other emotionally significant events, such as Vietnam, Kent State, Nixon's resignation, and so forth, shape individual behavior patterns.

Though the models are very broad, they do allow the interventionist to establish constructs relative to value sets held by people and the dynamics present within most organizations. One way of looking at an environment is as an arena for the collision of various value sets. Once you are able to smoke out the value sets in conflict, you can identify the lines of force behind them and are better able to identify appropriate, substitute ways of looking at the world.

The generational groupings below represent an elaboration upon Massey's original model updated and adapted for our use.

Beavis and Buttheadist   **The Board Member**

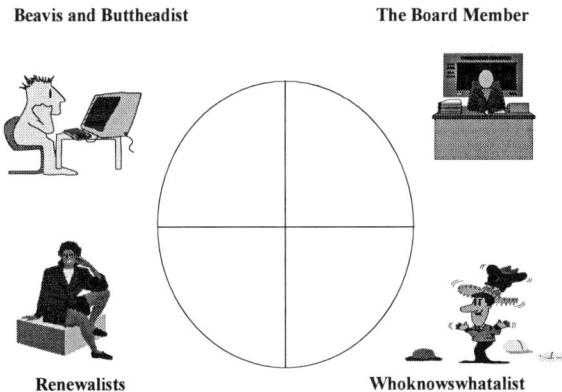

Renewalists   **Whoknowswhatalist**

The four groupings of people should be viewed as starting with the Board Member who was driven by the values inculcated in people by the Depression and World War II, to the Whoknowswhatalist as exemplified by those who were brought into Washington with Mr. Clinton to the Renewalists who have absolutely no way of understanding what the Board Member does and why he does it, and the Beavis and Buttheadists whom I honestly do not understand. It is important to keep in mind that the further the distance between the types, the more difficult it is to get them to the same place to understand each other and be able to communicate with each other in a meaningful way.

The Board Member

The Board Member is usually white and male. He is from 55 to 65 years old and is a firm believer in the Protestant work-ethic. He believes that hard work and fundamental values are what made this country great. He tends to think of things bipolarly--yes or no, good or bad, black or white. He looks back to World War II as the "Big One" and he yearns for a future time when values were as clear as they were back then. The Board Member believes in the family, sees religion as a critical component of our value systems, and believes that if the employees work hard for the organization, the organization should take care of them. The Board Member understands the messages that the Depression sent us--hard work, thrift, and preparedness for disaster; he believes that these values are all keys to our success. The Board Member is a left side of the brain kind of person; he appreciates logic, rational behavior, documentation of rules in manuals, and is repulsed by reports that contain anything other than the "facts."

W h o k n o w s w h a t a l i s t

Ws are very confused. Ws are either male or female. They are well educated, but their education has taught them to be even more questioning and equivocal in their answers--the result of which is that they appear to be confused. Ws are somewhere between 40 and 55 and thrive in ambiguity. They tend to be process oriented rather than to focus upon obtaining closure on anything. They very much enjoy status but their leadership style is masked within a complicated and cumbersome process--they want feedback on what they are thinking. Therefore, they tend to spend more time in thinking than in getting things done; they are big in obtaining consensus. One never knows which side of an issue Ws will come down on and neither do Ws. They see everything as gray and nothing as black and white.

On the one hand, Ws share some of the Depression era values of the Board Member and, on the other, they find them horribly materialistic. When staying at hotels, a W might well take an extra bar of soap home with them but their intent would be to give it to someone more needy than them if the need arises; in fact, they won't give it away until their total collection starts mildewing or starts blocking doorways. They have fascinating explanations for their decisions and actions because they sincerely can see multiple sides of any issue.

Renewalists

The Renewalists are from 25 to 40 years old. They don't quite know what they stand for but they are adamant in their belief that it is not the same as the Board Members; they feel that the Board Members are off in right field. They do not look at family, religion, or Depression values as the core of their being. They share some of the confusion of the Ws but they feel separated from them by the fact that they do not think their world is gray; they believe in a black and white world.

The core characters who populate Seinfeld represent this group. Kramer, George, and Elaine each represents their own eccentricity that they believe in firmly; Jerry spends his time making these eccentricities visible to others. Jerry seems angry about how the world works but we never really know why; he has a beef of some kind but it tends to be general rather than specific. Clearly, all four treasure their outside of work activities; both Kramer and George appear to be unemployed and there appears to be little stigma associated with that.

Beavis and Buttheadist

This group is from 18 to 25 years old. Their labeling is not to make the pejorative judgment that they are substantially like the two cartoon characters. What the label does suggest is that this group's values change very rapidly, almost in a stream of consciousness way. They have been bombarded with so many changes in the external world as communicated to them through the media that they have a difficult time in defining who they are in the present. Whereas the Ws were confused relative to whether they were Traditionalists or Renewalists, the BB's are confused relative to everything. This group has learned that the relative economic security of working for a paternalistic US company is a thing of the past, they understand that their lives in all likelihood will be less prosperous than their parents, and they feel that they have lost context.

The Dynamics

These four value sets create interesting dynamics when put into play within the organizational context. Questions that the interventionist might ask when using the models in the field might include the following:

1. When Board Directives come down, how are they made relevant to the B&Bs? Are their messages articulated in a fashion that even register with the stream of consciousness type processing of the information by the BBs?

2. What role do the Ws have in bridging the gulf of dissonance between the Board Members and the Renewalists/B&Bs? What role can they be facilitated

into playing? If the Board Members are out of   touch
with what is going on in the environment, how   does
the organization bring them into touch or   buffer
their   isolation   from   the   other   groups   without
threatening their positions of authority? What happens
to Ws when they move from a position of weighing all
options and not executing very much and become true
leaders who spend less time in analysis? How do the
Renewalists react? How do the Board Members? If an
individual comes to interview for a position, which of
the four roles would be the most   effective in getting
them hired?

3. How does the organization develop policy and
practice so that the generational value sets are best
accommodated? How has the organization evolved to
take into account that much of the organization's
infrastructure has been built upon Board Members'
beliefs systems that have almost no relevance to the
Renewalists and B&Bs?

4. How can acculturation of all groups occur so that the
complexity of value sets held by each of the four
groups   can   create   organizational robustness, and
synergy?

Application: Generational Model

When working with a new group of clients, initiate the
session with a discussion of the multitude of values held by
members of the culture. In a manufacturing setting, clients
will identify different types of individuals who populate third
shift than those who populate days or seconds. In government,
some folks well might identify that 80% of the federal worker
population coasts and have no commitment to work except for
their paychecks while 20% are the go-getters who work hard
for personal gratification. Any other number of possibilities
can be worked.

Once the group really does focus upon their organization
as types of individuals, rather than as an amorphous blob
where no differentiation can take place, you can begin
working on the above model. Breaking the group into four and

having each team work on one quadrant of the circle and then report back to the group results in some intellectually provocative insights and an enjoyable learning experience.

2. The Spherical Model

Our culture reinforces certain types of behaviors more than others. Though our culture handsomely rewards creativity at the highest levels--Spielberg's *Schindler's List,_* Pei's design of the pyramid entrance to the Louvre,_ Perlman's performance on the violin, it in general does not encourage creativity in management nor in management consultants. In fact, both management and management consultants are expected to be pretty flat, unimpressive, overly analytical types generally incapable of leading others or themselves into the new. All too often, business enterprises encourage analysis, quantitative thinking, and written reports that have been scrubbed of all traces of feeling. For most clients, the cry from the organization's middle is: "We have no vision around here, let alone strategy." Vision is the antithesis of analysis.

Civilization has nurtured within us a duality. On the one hand, we have a predisposition for wanting equilibrium and balance. On the other, we want to throw off the shackles of conformity and to break out and experience the titillating and the bizarre. Western art has manifested this duality very clearly throughout the 2500 year battle between Classicism and Romanticism. This same battle is being waged now within enterprises that articulate a need for change.

One can literally go through civilization's bipolar ways of looking at the world by going through the Art Museum of any major city. As you meander from room to room your psyche becomes overwhelmed as you move from the Graeco-Roman traditions to those of the Middle Ages to those of the Renaissance to the Baroque to the Neo-Classical to the Romantic. To keep from becoming overwhelmed by the enormity of the dissonance of the styles, individuals focus upon their "likes" by categorizing and limiting what they will see on a given day--an attempt for them to maintain equilibrium of civilization's duality within them.

The Classical traditions of which we are a part gave birth to the brilliance of the Parthenon, of a Monticello, of the works of a Beethoven and a Moliere, all the way through and including the serenity enveloped in the design of Chicago's Soldier's Field. Classical artists and designers alike created their work within very clear cut parameters that included balance, symmetry, and predictability. They focused upon the humanity of us all and they celebrated our control over the unknown and the unrefined.

A wonderful example of the same is Michelangelo's *David*. The visitor to Florence walks down a long hall populated by chunks of stone which Michelangelo began carving and then discarded in his search for *"The David."* Each is remarkable in its own way until one reaches the end of the hall and experiences the masterpiece; all one can hear are the clicks of cameras. There are no voices; individuals from all countries stand with mouths agape, drinking in the power of the work. They just stand and watch as if the thousands of pounds of serenity is about to move from his pose and saunter off down the hallway.

David is physiologically stunning in its perfection, but is much more. It reflects the serenity of Michelangelo, the Classical humanist, who carved the spirit of the time into a form that all could understand. *David* is larger than life, but his serenity of spirit is not. He stands there with sling in hand after doing battle and he seems oblivious to the evisceration and death around him. The artist captured *David*'s spirit all right, the one filtered through the lens of a Classical humanist's eye and which emanates the confidence, serenity, balance and symmetry of an individual who had mastered his environment.

At the other end of this duality, is the Romantic spirit that appears to be restively under control in each of us but which bubbles beneath the surface like molten lava waiting to erupt into consciousness and beyond. The Romantic heritage gave birth to the bizarre visions of Bosch, of the ghosts, witches, and insanity in the works of Shakespeare, in the paintings of Goya and Delacroix, and the design of the Victorian Mansion.

The research into what mode most CEOs operate is very conclusive. If an individual has been trained as an engineer, an accountant, a financial analyst, or a computer programmer, they almost always will require intellect and order to rule all. If they have been trained in the social sciences or the humanities or on the shop floor, they will focus more upon intuition and a human network to help them in their decision making. In the abstract, neither way of thinking is preferable within an industrial or service setting. When at the cusp of organizational and cultural change, it is imperative that the change facilitator be able to intervene in such a way that a significant shift from the intellectual to the intuitive take place.

The chances are high that at the time of intervention, the CEO, the Program Sponsor, and the individuals selected for the team are going to have roughly the below balance of the left and right sides of the brain.

Imbalances in Spherical Function

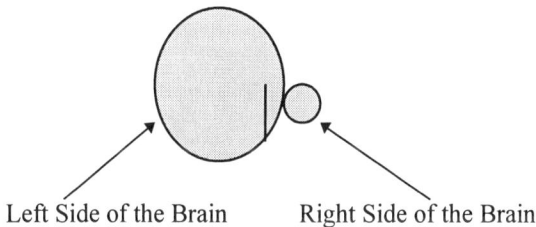

Left Side of the Brain   Right Side of the Brain

Application: Spherical Function

When entering into the client environment for the start of a change process, initial interviews will indicate some of the values of the organization as well as those kinds of behaviors that are rewarded. Almost always there is a true resistance to moving forward to get things done. Even though few would expect anything other than radical change as being the goal the process, individuals driven by the left sphere of the brain try to make the process incremental in nature. Common excuses for creeping incrementalism include: Not enough data being collected, unavailability of the appropriate resources to get the work done, lack of available time to get it done right, events X and Y are going to happen which would make real organizational change a success, and there is no executive leadership. It is critical to keep in mind that all of these excuses, in all likelihood, are used as strategies for risk minimization; this risk minimization is something encouraged and reinforced by the enterprise so should be taken as a closely held belief. There is never a perfect time to begin a change effort and many situations that present themselves have been worked through somewhere by someone else.

It is not suggested that we can provide step by step instructions for migrating from the left sphere of the brain to the right. There are some tools provided by first rate business process re-engineering methodologies for doing so. Each contains a step of activity where one *challenges* everything that they have done for the value stream under consideration and then the team comes up with a *vision* for which it will work. The vision, in particular, is rooted in radical change.

For instance if the time involved in processing a purchase order is currently 82 days, the vision would be for it to be two days. It is relatively easy, though a bit painful, to get a group to sign up to such a degree of risk. What is facilitated here is the left sphere types being coached to stretch so far that they realize that the stretch is not really a risk at all. Who would not want their cycle time to be two days rather than 82? Moving in this direction tends to liberate folks from their left sphere into the right and back into the left for practically getting the job done.

It is of note that clients who have immersed themselves in Total Quality Management Teams sign up for their first team and will rarely go onto a second; those who do organizational change activities once search for opportunities for more. Though the experience is very demanding and at times painful, individual growth almost always occurs for those who invest in the process.

Facilitator Notes

1. The mode of operating primarily in the intellectual mode is the programming of an individual by the business

enterprise; the programming can be reversed, even though our objective is not do so. Our objective is not to violate the cultural dictates of the organization in which we are working but is to allow these individuals to move back and forth between the two modes without causing them significant discomfort.

2. It is likely that individuals weighted heavily on the left side of the brain at work do not necessarily operate solely in that mode outside the office. It is quite likely that they have learned the social acceptability of being a robot-like individual at work but are quite different playing sports, interacting with their family and working in service to their church or synagogue.

3. Though it is fine for individuals to operate in the well-developed left side of the brain modality sometimes and to operate in the well-developed right side of the brain in others, it is a very different thing for individuals to ignore the need for balance between the two. Individuals who restrict how they operate deprive themselves of the tools needed to look at any phenomenon from a multi-faceted perspective that will hurt them eventually professionally and will create dysfunctionality with them and the ones whom they care for personally.

4. In accerbation of the problem, all too many business change consultants come to the table with the same imbalance as that of the clients whom we wish to migrate from old ways of perceiving and behaving. They have a very difficult time in ever understanding what needs to be done to begin the migration. Rather than looking into areas that they do not know, they dive deeply into minutiae to generate spreadsheets, graphs, models, documents, and assorted other forms of security and shelfware. The end-sum of their consulting work is that the sponsor sends them packing and they leave bitter towards the experience and the client.

3. The Business of Stories

> The world that we have made as a result of the level of
> thinking we have done thus far creates problems that we
> cannot solve at the same level we created them at.
>
> Albert Einstein

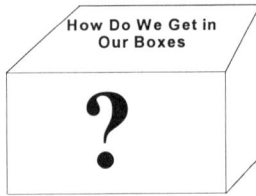

How Do We Get in
Our Boxes

?

Research into the perceptual worlds of the very young has
revealed that they see a world of possibility, teeming with
things that they cannot wait to explore. Toddler's hands and
mouths seek out everything to embrace and engulf. As they sit
in their cribs or playpens everything is potentiality; they
aggressively pursue these phenomena when the opportunity
presents itself.

This exploratory state exists also when mature individuals
take on a position of employment with a company that is
unfamiliar to them. It is remarkable how open-minded and
enthusiastic employees are during their first ninety days. Even
a few long-tenure folks have the knack of always retaining
their enthusiasm, even for decades!

However, in both of our populations, this urge for action is
interrupted by that all too familiar reality principle that
dampens enthusiasm. Someone in a position of authority steps
in and quashes the exploratory impulse. Paradoxically, both
the parent and the boss who can benefit their organizations
most by nurturing exploration and motivation spend their time
in restricting it to the point that it is strangled. It is critical that
we examine some fundamental phenomena that occur in both
situations but which we will face as we intervene in situations.

In the child's case, as she progresses through interacting
with her environment, she will be told in a variety of fashions

that she is not to pull on the lamp cord. She might be told by precept and admonition: "No, Susan! Don't you dare touch that or I'll slap your hand!" Or she might be informally coached or presented models where the message is more subtle, but there nevertheless. Or the parent can go through a very technical description of all the ins and outs of engaging in what the parent describes as inappropriate behavior.

In the new employee's case, the enthusiasm quashing can take any number of forms. Peer pressure might tell the employee that people who try to show up their fellow employees are really not team players. The worker might discover that no matter what they do, their compensation will be the same. The employee might become disenfranchised because the boss does not really seem to care about the contribution that this person is making. Very few organizations encourage and nurture breaking out of the box, although many have programs that they maintain in a token fashion for that very purpose, e.g., suggestion system programs, innovation awards, and recognition for TQM achievements.

How we got in the box (maybe)

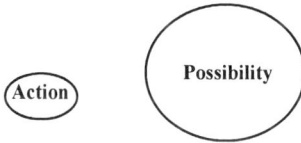

Research has revealed that when individuals strive hard for the achievement of their possibility or goal and when actions by others--actions which the perceiver senses are unjust--interfere with the achievement of that goal, they react in one of the following fashions:

1. They do not in any way let the occurrence affect them and they prepare to meet their next challenge;

2. They react emotionally to the injustice and protect themselves by closing down avenues for exposure for additional hurt;

3. They forget all about additional avenues of opportunities and ascribe stories to the action that begin to take on a life of their own.

This business of stories requires critical focus on the part of the interventionist. At the very core of the story is the fact that by its very nature it is delusional--an individual is shocked, traumatized or deeply hurt by something in his/her environment. Rather than accepting the fact that all of these things occur in life and recognize that the corresponding pain goes with the territory of living a full life, the individual denies that fact and substitutes a story. The story provides delusional comfort that will prevent healing since recognition of the disease is a pre-requisite to its cure. Please note that it is not suggested that people who develop stories are bad or sick people; everyone makes up stories occasionally. What is critical to keep in mind is that one of our primary responsibilities as interventionists is to gently encourage folks to acknowledge the need to unravel their stories related to the work place and to replace *thanatos*--death oriented--stories with *eros*--life oriented ones.

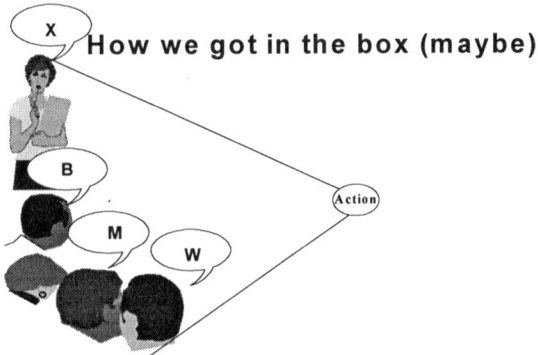

How we got in the box (maybe)

What is critical in our considerations is the fact that, all too often, there is a substantial disconnect between an action relating to the exploration of the world and perceived opportunities for getting ahead. Individual A says X to get Y result and they get F. Not only do they get F but because of the emotion surrounding the event, receivers of the X message perceive X and F as indeed being W, M, and B.

The following three cases exemplify the pathological nature of stories:

Case 1

Sean Hogan was a Principal Consultant with a Big Six consulting firm. In his rise to that position, he was always respectful of others and was the life of a cocktail party. He never rubbed anyone the wrong way.

Sean was an engineer by training, as his father before him. He had suffered during school and throughout much of his career because he had a difficult time learning, and his overbearing super-engineer of a father had not helped the situation--he was always putting pressure on him and talking about when he was a student. As an undergraduate he expected to fall in the footsteps of his vision of his dad who worked 40 hours a week while taking eighteen hours of classes a semester and who, as his father would tell it, became recognized internationally as a super-engineer.

Instead of meeting that vision, Sean had started as an electrical engineering student, moved to mechanical engineering, and then said that he moved to industrial engineering. In fact, he had moved into industrial management that was not engineering at all but he never had the nerve to tell his overbearing father. His father still treated him as if he were a kid.

When one of the Big Six partners in Sean's practice had a heart attack, Sean was promoted to an associate partner. Rather than taking on the pleasant and somewhat tenuous demeanor that had carried him up to that point in time, Sean was at a loss for how to act. He was very insecure about how to act and would not trust his past personality for fulfilling the responsibilities that faced him currently.

Lacking confidence in who he was, Sean became what he perceived to be his infallible father, with all of the commensurate obnoxiousness and overbearing behavior that characterized him. He would berate others, would visit clients and feign that he knew what their problems were without them even articulating them. He seemed to take pleasure in running roughshod over others, just as his father had run over him. In essence, all of those around Sean learned to hate him just as Sean had learned to hate his father, only to create his version of his father that became a myth who lived him.

Facilitator's Notes

It is unimportant what the nature of the relationship was between Sean and his father. It is clear that during data collection in the environment that Sean is damaging it and those who work within it with him. It is highly unlikely that Sean will ever come clean regarding his fantasy about who he is.

What can be provided to him by the consultant is the fact that benchmarked executives have certain manners of behavior with others and that few of theirs correspond to what Sean was manifesting. Sean needs to be provided with a series of feedback instrument results that show him how he ranks relative to his peers and then be provided with a series of alternative models from which he can choose. When individuals, who do not suffer from severe mental illness pathologies, act in fashions which alienate them from significant numbers of others around them, they do so because of the lack of a broad range of models that they can follow and their incapacity to identify the feedback from others which indicates a need for change.

Case 2

In fact, Al was a super engineer. He had gone to the best schools and had received numerous awards for his outstanding scholarship. When he went out into the world of manufacturing, he excelled in each area of engineering that he worked. At a very early age, 28, he was appointed as the Engineering Director of a very large manufacturing facility.

Though Al was an exceptional engineer, his education was very restricted. As an undergraduate he never took a writing, literature, or social studies course. He never attended cultural events more sophisticated than Bruce Willis movies. He had very little exposure to dating since he was perceived as a geek by women on the outside of work and inside work he hung around with his fellow engineers who were obnoxious, bordering on cultish.

As talented as Al was, he started having problems at work. Whereas, his model for behaving was that of the super engineer--efficient and to the point, others kept seeking a bit of humanity beneath his gruff exterior. He was very focused upon getting almost immediate closure on everything and if someone was more process oriented, he would let then know immediately that he absolutely had no respect for them. He could not understand why the "sensitives" around him could not get to work and cut all the warm and fuzzy stuff.

(Al's dysfunctional story was that the engineering model is the one that, not only he, but everyone else in the world should follow. It was a clear, crisp way of processing the world, from his view. The difficulty is that by failing to understand the way in which others process their world, he becomes dysfunctional with them and insensitive to what motivates them. It is very dangerous for a manager to be in this position. Fortunately, there are thousands of models of migration from super-engineering to balance by individuals similar to Al. The interventionist again needs to hold the mirror up to Al's environment and work with him in making his story a bit less superficial.)

Case 3

By all accounts, Ginger did not have an easy life. Her mother left her family when she was three. She was raised by her siblings; she always felt alone. Her books and her fantasies were the only true companions that she had.

Ginger developed a story that life was impossible, that sadness was a part of everything, and she committed herself to never letting anyone into her real world where they might run across her sadness and pain. Accompanying her story was the development of a passive aggressive personality where she feigned acceptance of everything and everyone and then undercut such positions with derision and cynicism, which left people who thought she was their friend angry and resentful.

Ginger was very talented but her story kept alienating her from others. Professionally, she could always make it to the level below "officer," but she never could become one. The fact that she had been passed over several times for important positions only made her more angry and her hostility became deeper and more damaging to others. It got to such a point that she became severely depressed whenever she was not at work but was able, on the surface, to be doing quite well at work. Outside of work, she lived in a hell that she created for herself. That of course was the self-fulfilling story she lived to fill.

(Unfortunately, there are many Gingers out there who act counter-productively to fulfill their self-prophecy of pain. They tend to gravitate to enterprises whose goals are relatively weak and, therefore, that tolerate anti-productive behavior. As an interventionist, passive-aggressives must be recognized early and worked with hard to prevent them from sabotaging the intervention. Fortunately, these folks are quick to acknowledge their passive-aggressive tendencies--they sometimes even think that they are funny, and can be turned around into model team participants.)

The Elephant in the Center of the Dining Table

When family units have something within their environment that they do not want to acknowledge, they often create a story that it is not there. A friend of mine describes it as if an elephant were sitting in the middle of the dining room table but no one says anything about it. Examples include an alcoholic whose problem is never acknowledged, a teenager who has gone out of control, all the way to a group of individuals who are being discriminated against and which others ignore.

Considering that most individuals learn their business behavior in some form of family unit, they carry the story of "its invisible" with them. There is a tendency for everyone to avoid confrontation and redirection of Sean, Al or Ginger above, because all too often their story is that one does not go looking for trouble. The net result of this learned behavior is that not only the individual who is dysfunctional causes difficulties but these dysfunctionals tend to bring out the dysfunctionalities of the supposed non-dysfunctionals-- dysfunctionality is laid upon dysfunctionality to such a degree that when the interventionist walks into the job she oft times thinks that she entered Dante's *Inferno*.

It is up to the interventionist to diagnose, reflect back to the entire culture what patterns of behavior are occurring, and to move the members of the team to a set of realities that they subliminally acknowledge but have difficulties in contending with the challenges.

Client Situation 1

Entrance into the client site revealed a team of well-educated R&D professionals in a state of chaos. There were multi-dimensional wars going on in the team and no one knew from day to day what new alliances would form and what old ones would disintegrate. At the center of chaos was the Team Leader--Joe--who, though extremely bright, clearly could be seen as the problem. Joe never stopped talking. He would be asked a simple question and he was off on one of his tirades. If he were asked how many dollars were available to do a project, he would explain the evolution of money.

The net effect of Joe's behavior was paralysis of the team; they did not even aspire to productivity. Joe spent a great deal of his time focusing upon all of the team conflict; he felt a great deal of satisfaction in intervening in the various spats that evolved. 98% of all words spoken were by Joe.

Client Situation 2

Ross was the Manager of a very large manufacturing operation in the Southwest. There were 1800 people who worked at the plant and depended upon their employment there because there were few other opportunities in the area. Manufacturing costs were high at the Plant and everyone there knew that if something were not done in the immediate future to increase productivity, there was a good chance that the facility would close.

Ross's relationships with his peers were very poor. He had been appointed to the position over several candidates in the plant who thought they could do a better job. Objectively, they probably could have. Ross had absolutely no manufacturing experience. He had started his career with the Company as a gopher, moved into special projects, and eventually landed in Accounting. In fact, sentiment was that Ross had only one thing going for him--the Group President doted upon him. Ross and he would spend half an hour each day on the phone with Ross giving him the latest confidentialities that had been shared with him. When other managers confronted Ross with his indiscretions, he just let out a high pitched giggle and went waddling down the hall, oblivious to the anger of those around him.

When planning was initiated for cutting costs, the worst of Ross emerged. When they had to consider how much to cut, Ross would push for more and more. He was always overruled by the managers, but he then called the Group President who would miraculously dictate the exact numbers that Ross specified. Morale was at an all time low among the management team; there were rumors on the floor that Ross was going to be killed.

Client Situation 3

Jill ran a Management Information Systems shop for a major banking conglomerate. Jill had a reputation of being tough, aggressive, and swift to act. If you messed with Jill you knew that she would not react immediately, but wait until the time was right where she would eviscerate you in front of individuals who mattered. People did not want to work with her or be on her teams because she was perceived as gutting folks just for the fun of it. If she did not get an opportunity each week, she would be missing something. People did not mess with Jill; they did not work with her either.

The *Eros/Thanatos* Continuum

In each of the three cases identified above, for apparently unknown reasons, the behaviors of individuals are retarding the total productivity of a unit and negative things are displacing the positive. Why is it that Joe's monopolization was allowed to destroy the productivity of the team as well as fragment it into the destructive alliance *du jour*? Why could not a group of grown adults stop Ross in his tracks from going to the Group President with every tidbit that he could to undercut the power of the team? Why would a sophisticated organization allow Jill the Knife to do her damage?

Each of the above has their own unique histories that significantly predispose them to specific kinds of behavior; this behavior is shared among each of the three folks who fall under an umbrella of being impacted by those who were *thanatos* driven and influenced. The fact that the individuals around them cannot modify their behavior significantly draws them into the *thanatos* vortex also. This gets us back to this business of stories that we need to explore even further.

Those who are *thanatos* driven push others towards death rather than its opposite of life--*eros*. They thrive upon the destruction of others and, of course, would not recognize the fact themselves. The very subtle messages that they send out to their young are subconsciously stored away as a tape which in all likelihood will wreak very serious damage upon the psyche of the young person.

It is hypothesized that each of the three individuals is being driven by a story that has displaced the reality of an action and has become a sustaining fantasy. Jungian Psychologists describe the phenomenon as the myth living you rather than you living the myth. The main characters in each of our six cases have substituted a new reality from that objectively identifiable in the external environment and each has embraced it totally.

Each of them acts in a fashion which on the surface might appear to get them ahead, but which will ultimately lead to their own destruction. When one violates the trust, confidence and self-respect of others, one releases forces of destruction that though sometimes slow to act, they act conclusively.

For instance, Joe's behavior of unilaterally addressing everything under the sun to keep the focus upon himself resulted in his isolation from the rest of the group and in their non-functioning; self-centeredness destroys any possibility of teaming and results in the individual's isolation from the realities of the workplace. Ross's non-chalant violation of confidences and trust created anger throughout the plant.

One destructive act has a ripple effect upon all the individuals around it. If others around the original actor have a predisposition for the same death seeking behaviors, with momentum and support it can parallel the development of the culture that degenerated into that of   Nazi Germany. Superficially Jill was a team player; her need to destroy, rather than maturely reaching compromises with those who might have inconvenienced her, in all likelihood will destroy her career in the long term--that which you reap, you sow.

The *thanatos* drive is not something that is heinous and hideous and preconceived by the individual being driven by it. It is a set of beliefs that becomes more and more isolated from reality--from any kind of anchoring action, and the individual pulls further and further from others because they appear to the driven to a superficially rooted sense of security that they have in their fantasy world.

The Eros/Thanatos Vortex

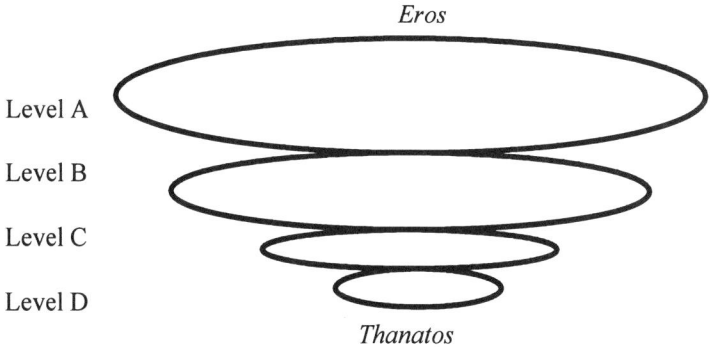

Eros

Level A

Level B

Level C

Level D

Thanatos

The Vortex resembles a tornado but it operates in reverse. At its opening at its top, it has a mouth that works to draw in individuals who are predisposed to a *thanatos* orientation. As the individuals are drawn in from Level A they move down until they are at Level D where they can rarely escape.

Outside the Vortex, individuals strive to push themselves away from death-like activity and decomposing life by pushing them up away from the Vortex to *eros*. The *eros/thanatos* continuum is not focused solely on where individuals fall on it but also upon how an entire institution goes about reinforcing what it considers to be the appropriate behaviors. If the institution systemically avoids bureaucracy, if it is flexible, if it attracts and keeps the best available talent, and if it makes the individuals within the organization into a synergized team of winners, it, and most of the individuals within it, are on the move towards *eros*. If an organization is hierarchically organized where bureaucrats frustrate employees needs to get at resources, if cycle times for reacting to the marketplace are twice what they should be, if issues relating to sexual harassment and maintenance of the dignity of employees are focused upon in discussions in breakrooms and lunchrooms, and if most employees go to work to make money rather than to move towards self-actualization, then it is rooted in a drive towards *thanatos*.

A Vortex Study

The Amish family settled during the late 1800's on an eight square mile section of land in the Great Plains of the United States. They grew and prospered because of their hard work and because of the mutual support provided by the community. Each day the men would go outside to work behind their mule or team of horses and the women would spend their time with their responsibilities and taking care of the children. Everyone in the community knew their place and they did not want to become involved much with those different from them.

Things went relatively well for the community until the 1970's. One hundred years of dividing the land into smaller and smaller pieces for the sons born of families resulted in the pieces getting too small to sustain a family. The children had never known anything different from their lifestyle, and that of generations before them, so they tried to keep their traditions as long as possible. It made no sense for them to make money on the land away from their community; they lived for their context.

When lands were divided more and more, it became inevitable that some of the young men had to go to the factories to provide for their families. When they arrived they did not see sunshine, they were isolated from nature, and others felt a hostility towards them because they were different. They did not care to be in an environment of solvents and dust and they did not adapt at all well to the technology. It was a common occurrence to see tears running down the dust covered faces of individuals who were fighting fiercely to keep from being ingested by the vortex.

Another Possible Explanation: A Model

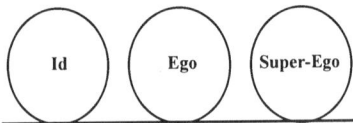

We have used models as tools to explore unobtrusively how cultures are constructed relative to their systems of beliefs and we have been focusing upon the individual dimensions within those same cultures. Sigmund Freud left us with a set of tools that assists us in supporting the fine tuning of belief systems within cultures and in optimizing individual contributions to its success. Because of some of the misunderstandings, and just plain distortions, of Freud's work, it is imperative that we define those dimensions of his work that have been shown to be successful by interventionists in the past.

We will restrict our considerations to three central components of Freud's model--the id, the ego, and the super-ego. Our use of these models will be to attempt to identify those psychological components that drive each of the individuals within the environment that we are exploring so that we can then accelerate the development of the individuals. It is critical to note that our observations can be obtained relatively rapidly through indirect observation of our clients, and because of the non-obtrusive approach, the individuals will not feel that their space is being violated.

Freud believed that the psyche was a closed system. He believed that whenever a phenomenon was processed by an individual, there was a change in the ratios of the various components of the psyche. He believed that some components in an individual were developed fully and that some needed opportunities for remedial growth. Unfortunately, if growth did not happen when it happens with most individuals, the remedial growth might be excruciatingly difficult to facilitate.

The Id

The id is the storehouse of energy for the psyche. It powers its two siblings--the ego and the superego. However, there is also an incredible dependency present between the driver and those systems that are driven.

The id goes on rampages. It is compulsive. It wants everything and it wants it now. If it had to be characterized as residing in a character, George Constanza's character in Seinfeld has strong manifestations of idish behavior.

George's id is not tempered by his ego and his super-ego. Whereas the id is a driver of uncontrolled wonts, the ego is the reality principle that kicks in to satisfy a need. For instance, if the id identifies a need for sex, it creates for itself an image that becomes its own reality, irrespective of its rootedness in the real world. Fantasy is the id's only reality--a reality that often is fleeting because the id will create as many fantasies as it needs so that its energies can be expended. The difficulty with this phenomenon is that the id, by itself, cannot get any satisfaction.

In George's case, he never receives satisfaction of his sexual drive. One memorable example was the episode where he is involved in a relationship with a woman whom he apparently cares for a great deal, or so he tells us. Of course, being the idish driven character that he is, he has never learned to temper his discussions with others regarding matters which most of us would consider intimate. In the restaurant where Seinfeld's friends meet, he discusses with Jerry his problems that he is having with having oral sex with his girlfriend. It is described by him as: "Anything down there south of the Equator is uncharted waters. Its unfamiliar terrain and anything can happen down there."

In the same episode, Elaine drives George's id into a frenzy by suggesting that women, especially her, fake climaxes on a regular basis. He becomes anxiety filled and disoriented. His entire sex life seems to pass in front of his eyes and he sees all women with whom he has been intimate as frauds and deceivers. His fantasy becomes his reality and he becomes compulsive about confirming his fantasies that he has just created about his new girlfriend. He layers this fantasy upon another fantasy *du jour* that he is impotent.

His entire reality, which could change completely when a different stimulus strikes it, is that he is sexually dysfunctional and that all the women in his life are frauds. After eating an aphrodisiacal mango, another of George's fantasies--this one suggested by Kramer, he loses his impotence by making love successfully with his partner. However, enveloped by his pride in his sexual performance, the energy that was invested in the impotence fantasy that has died, is invested in his other fantasy that his partner has been duplicitous. He believes that she is one with all other women who fake climaxes and he tells her the same. His partner becomes incredulous. Rather than following ecstasy with even a modicum of tenderness, he accuses. Understandably, she kicks him out of her bed and out of her life. George does not understand. He avoids the reality of the situation by ascribing evil to others rather than validating his rather bizarre observations. He believes that the reason for his loss of the girlfriend is that she realizes that he exposed her fraudulent behavior.

Additional sexual fantasies which never make it into the reality tempered world for George include his belief that the only way he can be satisfied sexually is to relate to women who hate him and basing all of his relationships on lies, e.g. telling one of his partners that he is a marine biologist, another that the reason he trampled her and small children on his way out of a burning room was the fact that he was demonstrating his heroic proclivities. As the embodiment of the id, he erupts into doing things without admitting the consequences for his actions.

The Ego

The ego is the reality principle of the psyche. It takes the aimless wonts of the id and identifies satisfiers for them. The satisfiers may or may not be acceptable to society so the influence of the super-ego interjects morality into the ego's deliberations. When operating optimally, the ego listens to the advice of the super-ego and takes a balanced perspective in providing id satisfaction. A strong ego tempers the overbearing super-ego.

A preponderance of large organizations today nudge individuals in the direction of an almost blind adherence to the dictates of those who embody the super-ego. Rules and regulations and adherence to speaking political correctness can lead the organization systemically to decline. Individuals who have strong egos and who can withstand such blind adherence should be recruited, placed, nurtured and rewarded for their independence and objectivity of thought.

The Super-Ego

The super-ego is the voice of society that tempers our actions. Whereas the id is the powerhouse of the psyche that needs to be channeled into acceptable behavior to meet its needs by the ego, the super-ego identifies whether the id and the ego are operating in the way that society wants.

For instance, the id is sent off into a flurry because of hunger. Left to its own way of doing things, it would flounder around directionless and never solve its hunger problem. In steps the ego, and communicates to the id that food is available and will solve the problem; the ego tells the id to go steal some food at the local grocery story. Neither the ego nor the id has a conscience. The super ego stops the id from stealing.

The difficulty with the super ego is that it is a controlling voice that, overdone, seriously hurts people's opportunities for self actualization. Specific examples include Woody Allen's mother as portrayed in his movies, the character on Friends who is played by Courtney Cox, and George Constanza's parents on Seinfeld. A little super-ego is fine, but more than enough paralyzes individuals into inactivity.

One model well worth exploration is that provided in Ken Kesey's *One Flew Over the Cuckoo's Nest*. McMurphy, an id driven entity par excellence, who has been newly introduced into a mental health institution, perceives the Big Nurse, who, for our purposes, can represent the embodiment of how culture addresses itself within super-ego types of forces to those who move into a state of disequilibrium and vulnerability; please note how the super-ego Nurse is perceived by McMurphy:

> She stops and nods at some of the patients, comes to and around   and stares out of eyes all red and puffy with sleep. She nods once to   each. Precise, automatic gesture. Her face is smooth, calculated and   precision made, like an expensive baby doll, skin like flesh colored enamel, blend of white and cream and baby blue eyes, small nose, pink little nostrils, everything working together except the color of her   lips and fingernails, and the size of her big bosom. A mistake was   made   somehow in manufactur-ing, putting those big, womanly, breasts   on   what would otherwise have been a   perfect work and you can see how bitter she is about it. (Kesey 1972, 5)

Ellis' Rational Emotive Psychotherapeutic Model

If we take all of the models that we have discussed up to now--Generational, Spherical Function, and Freudian, each of them shares one characteristic with the others--they all allow and, at times, support the individual by allowing them to evade the responsibility necessary to change. Within the Generational Model, you can hear the excuse: "I guess that some things that I picked up in the Sixties will never change." In the Spherical model: "I have spent so much of my time operating in the analytical mode that I guess visioning is just impossible for me." An individual like George Constanza in Seinfeld would not have the reflective disposition for questioning what he does in his persistent id state; an individual excessively influenced by the super-ego would be unable to do anything but ponder their past and reflect upon it, e.g., Woody Allen's movie characters.

At some point it is critical to move beyond analysis and into action with the therapeutic tools available that do not take a decade to learn. Albert Ellis has developed his Rational Emotive Psychotherapy tools that are as brilliant as they are simple. What Ellis' unique approach does is to shift the clients' participation in the change experience from whining to taking responsibility for their actions. In most interventions, clients are allowed to whine about their problems for too much of the engagement. (One of the groundrules that I have each team buy into early on is that no one is allowed to whine after the first half day of meetings.) Non-Ellis school's allow the client to escape from the responsibility associated with the ownership of change.

For example, therapy in the Rogerian School, that founded by an Ellis contemporary--Carl Rogers, is based upon the therapist giving positive, self affirming responses to the client. If a client was to say: "Upper leadership in this organization just does not want to take the lead." The therapist well might respond: "I see. You feel that leadership here just doesn't want to take the lead." The session might continue and the therapist would feel that the session was successful if the client threw off some frustrations and was able to see the kinds of things that were bothering her.

In Freudian Therapy, the therapist would attempt to have the client free associate with the contents of the messages that the client was making visible. "Upper leadership in this organization just doesn't want to take the lead." The therapist well might respond: "What makes you think that? That's very interesting. Have you seen this kind of thing before? What would you attribute this nervousness leading to." They would try to dig out as many things as possible from the client and then process them into an ever changing gestalt. Freudians explore beneath the immediate images generated by the client so that they can get at more profound truths than those which the client is willing to admit.

The Ellis' Therapist is only interested superficially in the client's state of uneasiness. They feel that the clients are living in their own stories and that they must jolt the client out of their whiny way of being. Ellis' Therapists are not focused upon being liked but of getting the client to develop. The first session most likely would go as follows:

Client: Upper leadership in this organization just doesn't want to take the lead.
Therapist: I understand that but so what? How does that possibly affect you?
Client: Well it affects me in that I can't do my job because we don't have the proper leadership to get things done, and I could lose my job is he doesn't get with it and do what he gets paid the big bucks for doing.
Therapist: And I guess that means that you are forced to sit there like a clod on the floor because the world can do things to you and you just plain don't have any resources to do anything about it. Maybe you'll allow vegetables to grow in you but otherwise you are a worthless clod.
Client: Wait a minute there. I never said I was a clod. I am really good at what I do and I am not a clod.
Therapist: Your message to me was that you are a worthless clod knocked down the hill by anything that came your way and that you are much more comfortable sitting here whining that doing anything about your ineffectuality.
Client: That is not what I said. What I mean is . . .
Therapist: Look, it doesn't really matter what you said. I appreciate it that you feel that there is no executive leadership and that it could affect you adversely. However, you are

pretending that that is someone else's problem and that the only thing that you can do is wring your hands. I need a commitment that you are going to quit whining, quit wringing your hands, and get off your butt. Word time is over, action time is here.

Client: You just don't understand the situation . . .

Therapist: Sure I understand the situation. Something is happening to you and you are not taking responsibility for stopping it to continue. You need to pull out your bag of skills and get going.

Client: So what do I need to do?

Therapist: See, there you go again. You are throwing responsibility for your plan back to me? Why don't you get some of your skin in the game?

Client: My skin?

Therapist: That's right, skin. Many of my clients come in here and they want to play only two of three roles. The roles are played by people at football games. The people in the stands play the role of yelling and screaming and carrying on and giving advice to the players, though they can't even see a whole lot about what is going on in the game. They even get a little liquored up and feel that their value to the players is increased. It's not. They do not accept responsibility.

The second role is played by the folks on the sidelines. They do not yell as much as the folks in the stands but they do have a sense that they are very close to the game. One of the reasons that they do not yell is that one of the players might take some exception to the advice. All in all, they do not have responsibility for anything, except for not being crushed on the sidelines.

And finally, we have the players themselves who are out there facing off against three hundred pound linemen who get their eyes poked, their knees twisted, their fingers broken--all because they are committed to following a plan for getting something accomplished, no matter how painful it is. They have invested. They are enrolled. They have skin in the game. Your job now is to quit talking and start walking. What kind of a plan can you put together for us to discuss during our next session.

Client: Well, I guess I'd have to think about it. Maybe I have been expecting for magic to happen. I will try and put something together.

Therapist: Excellent. It sounds as you want to take a bit more control of your life. See you next week.

Though we can use several tools for analysis, all that the analyses lead to is a designed plan for change. Ellis bridges the gap between the thinking and the doing and disciplines the client into developing responsibility and plans for action. We can assume that almost every client has a litany of excuses for things to remain the same. What we bring to the table are techniques for getting the client to get their skin in the change game.

Too much has been made of individuals not wanting to, or being ready for, change. Such perspectives are simply not validatable in the field. Individuals always have the kernels of change within them; cultures are the ones who retain their buffer zones. What individuals are almost always in desperate need of are the tools for change. A mechanic needs his tools, a teacher needs his. The above theories coupled with Ellis's simple technique provide the individual with the confidence needed to take on that which is uncertain.

Application: The Wayward Change Consultant.

The following is a composite model of a class of consultant out there who moves around the edges of facilitating organizational change, but avoids failure by avoiding substantial intervention and investment of skin. He then calls a failure a win.

Willy's High Tech Widgets Corporation

Willy's hired Martini and Ross Consultants to prepare them for some of the challenges that they knew they would be facing in the year 2000. Willy's was a very successful $50,000,000 a year Company that had been grown with venture capital to the point where they were doing quite well. Unfortunately, each year that went by, competitors took an additional chunk of what had originally been their market exclusively.

Martini and Ross send in their most senior partner to take a scan of the environment at Willy's. The partner is an accountant by training who migrated to systems work in the early Eighties. He determines that the best person to bring in to manage the project is Quentin Gray.

Quentin is fifty-five years old and has both a Bachelor's and Master's Degree in Computer Sciences. He thinks of himself as an engineer's engineer and for fun talks about *3rd level normal* and, with a glitter in his eye, *canonical synthesis*. Initially, Quentin usually is found to be absolutely loved by clients because of his non-abrasive style, his passivity, his technical knowledge, and his charm.

Quentin firmly believes that consultants have relative short life spans at clients. After several drinks, he has confided to his associates that clients: "First they want Quentin Gray," then they want someone "Like Quentin Gray," and then they ask: "Who is Quentin Gray." Quentin's history does follow that pattern; he is not loved towards the end of an engagement and almost never receives follow on work.

Quentin is called in to the office of the client, Jeanne Ortiz, a MIS person by training, who explains that the project does not have the proper context--that no one is on the same page. There is confusion in the executive team about what can be expected to come out of the project. One constituency thinks that the process is about saving money, another thinks it's about quality improvement, another thinks it's about improved customer satisfaction, another about organizational reinvention, and the Chief of Operations thinks it's about all of those things.

Quentin volunteers his service in sorting this out and agrees to work with Jeanne on it. He knows that he really has avoided these change things in the past, but, after all, he is really a smart person who is really good on his feet and this stuff has usually been left to human resources types of folks that he could not respect less. He knows that his firm has some expertise in this kind of stuff. He calls and finds that they would want about $50,000 to do a proper environmental scan and assessment. The project cannot afford it so he decides to do it himself.

Quentin starts attending one day workshops on facilitating change. He sits there and takes copious notes on topics such as: "Facilitating Organizational Change: The Ten Commandments for Success"; "Coping with Difficult People," and "The Psycho-Linguistic Programming Approach to Re-framing an Organization in Sixty Days." Quentin learns so much that he modifies his resume to show that he has 27 years of organizational change experience. He concludes that he has been doing this "change stuff" all along; he just never realized it.

Quentin puts together a plan. First he has to interview 18 people whom he has labeled as "stakeholders." Jeanne agrees to go with him on all of these interviews. Each interview is typed and put in a book on a shelf in the "team library." The interviews are synthesized and it is determined that there must be a vision. Quentin persuades Jeanne to schedule a visioning offsite for two days. Quentin is identified as the facilitator of the session.

All of the interviews are synthesized and are distributed to team members as pre-work. No specific comments can be traced to individuals. Quentin decides that this kind of work is really warm and fuzzy stuff and really relies upon the facilitator just kind of going with the flow. He has observed folks do this stuff and it has looked like a cake walk.

Eighteen individuals show up at the meeting. None of them are particularly thrilled about giving up their time to be there. There is a low level of anger in the air. Jelly roll chatter prior to the meeting encourages Quentin. He kicks it off by asking the question, which his production people have beautifully designed onto an easel pad flip chart:

"What would we all in this room have to do to win the Super-Bowl?"

Eyeballs roll; arms are crossed. People start looking at watches. Folks start making phone calls. Jeanne realizes that she is in deep trouble. Quentin does not know the people very well so he thinks things are going pretty well except for an impalpable something; he continues to be charming and then some.

Fred Glick interrupts Quentin's flow by asking: "Before you go much further there Mr. Gray, I would like to know what exact deliverables are Martini and Ross going to deliver here? You clearly are well meaning, but how can we justify the expense of doing this when all that we have received in the past from this kind of thing is another worthless thing the next year?"

Quentin remains poised. He immediately reverts to the project plan and leads the group into a fascinating discussion about information architectures. He demon-strates his mastery of the subject; towards the end of the day he even gets a round of discussion going about canonical synthesis.

He leaves the meeting invigorated by its success and reports back to his sponsors that everyone is now on board in moving towards a systematically designed information architecture.

Queries About Quentin

Unfortunately, too many people would look at the above situation and indicate that Quentin probably did a respectable job under the circumstances. They might suggest that he handled hostility relatively well; he turned negativity around into becoming something productive. To the contrary, Quentin's performance was deplorable.

Experience across a broad base of clients indicates that client expectations are so low in the area of change management that anytime something less than disaster occurs, they call it a win. Acceptance of Quentin's performance would suggest that his: ". . . if you get away alive with your hide you were great," attitude was very much in play

The following questions should be asked regarding Quentin's attitudes, skills, and abilities:

What specific models did he bring to the table, use in the analysis of the client group and use the data to modify his course of action?

How would you analyze Quentin with each of the models previously discussed in this chapter?

Is Quentin correct in his assumption that study of organizational change will allow the development of consulting skills in that area?

Is Quentin correct in that, in fact, he has been doing organizational change all along and the he simply had not realized it?

Is facilitating change a cake walk? If not, what kinds of activities could Quentin have engaged in to prepare him for the session?

How could Quentin have better identified the group dynamics at the beginning of the session?

What could he have done, specifically, to avoid getting off course in the first place?

What could Quentin do to redefine the impalpable something?

Why does Quentin avoid discussing a team vision and revert back to their project plan and information architectures?

Why does Quentin report back to his sponsors that he, indeed, has accomplished his objectives?

The New Jersey University Scenario

New Jersey University is a member of the Board of Governor's Colleges and Universities in the State of New Jersey; it is one of six sister schools in the State System. It does a good job of educating students in the most rural college in the Board of Governor's System.

Years ago, the BOG told NJU executives that it needed to develop a niche that differentiated it from the other BOG Schools. For instance, with reduced revenues available to the State, would not it make sense for NJU to drop courses that were available at Garden State University (part of the same system) located in Newark 50 miles away? Wouldn't it make sense to focus the state allocation on its areas of specialization? NJU had resisted such moves because of the turmoil it would create amongst faculty and staff.

NJU has experienced some of the same funding issues as those at other institutions of higher education throughout the United States. Twenty years ago it ran into big problems when it allowed capital expenditures to get out of line. An unexpected drop in revenue, as well as some questionable financial decisions, resulted in NJU's having to sell off assets to provide ample cash flow. The Legislature remembers NJU's mistakes and is not particularly sympathetic to their plight; besides, the urbanites who sit on the Education sub-committee have little patience with the problems with downstate rural folks; members have gone so far as to refer to NJU as the *utter* school.

During the current fiscal year, research funds were reduced because of a scandal related to how expenditures were accounted for in a major bovine research study. The federal government got word of the scandal and balked at continuing the same funding levels as in recent years, unless NJU was willing to maintain records to the intent and letter of accounting policies and procedures.

NJU has been underfunded by the State for three consecutive years. The faculty has become demoralized because of a two year freeze on wages; they feel that they have been milked for every bit of energy that they have within them. A new President--Jerome   Vinson, has been appointed, but there is cynicism regarding what he can do about their institution's plight; there is a sense that he is not a dig in his heels, "get NJU what it deserves," kind of guy. After all, the Board of Governors appointed him to the Presidency; he must have told them that hew was "flexible" regarding what it was entitled to receive. (In addition, the President's daughter was overheard at the local McDonalds as saying that her family could not stand it there)   Another prevailing theory is that NJU is perceived by the Legislature as not providing ample direction to faculty and not holding them accountable for productivity.

NJU has big problems with the age of its faculty and with some of their productivity. 81% of them are at the full professor level, 15% are at the associate professor level, 2% are assistant professors, and 2% are instructors. All but 5% are tenured--a result of having almost no turnover over the years because of the quality of life in rural Collegetown, comments of city dwellers notwithstanding.

In fact, there is a trend for some faculty members to almost double their income by running housing business for students; the faculty members rent to students and spend their free time maintaining the buildings. The downside of this, as well as the University's focus upon teaching and not research, is that when faculty are not teaching, they are not necessarily doing research or service either. The students tend to be a rather docile lot so there is even a question of whether much is going on in the area of teaching; each year for the past five years, fewer NJU alumni have been hired within six months of graduating than the previous year. Efforts to hold faculty accountable for carrying their fair share of workload have been reacted to violently by their union--UPUNJ (University Professor's Union of New Jersey, AFL/CIO).

On the whole, the faculty are demoralized. They feel that they have suffered decades of neglect by the Legislature and they feel that they have been stuck with a series of non-leaders in the management ranks. Paradoxically, the faculty wants strong leaders but when even marginally strong leaders have tried to take the lead at the University, faculty have resisted and resented the leadership because it was an infringement upon their rights of academic freedom. Actually, management is also demoralized because they think that faculty members are pulling with them and all of a sudden they find out in round-a-bout ways that the faculty are not supporting them.

For instance, Vinson had a meeting with the Chairperson of the Faculty Senate who agreed to facilitate consensus building in the Senate on a major, new Vinson initiative; not only did the Chair support Vinson, they ate dinner together and empathized with each others past and present research interests. They had actually agreed to have their families go skiing together within the month. Two days after the friendship was struck up, Vinson was told by his administrative assistant that the Chair's administrative assistant had overheard the Chair commenting to several faculty members that Vinson was focused only upon political expediency in moving on to his next job and that intellectually he was a lightweight.

Middle to lower level management within the University are irate. They do not feel that they are getting a fair deal from the University. They never get to go to training courses to help them obtain the tools to manage better. Any development they get, they pay for themselves. There is never reinforcement by the top of behaviors that they learn or is there even a feigned interest in the fact that they are developing. They feel that things never change at NJU and they focus upon extra-University activities rather than attempting to obtain satisfaction from their jobs.

The same group's annual reviews are horrible--they have evolved into being "happy talk" discussions where they are not given constructive feedback; the University has a tradition of never getting confrontational with non-performers or even dealing with individuals who need sincere feedback. The result is a sense of non-accountability. Generally, if you are quiet and docile, you keep out of trouble at NJU.

Annual reviews of staff management rarely result in performance reward. Most of management, as well as most other staff personnel, are maxed out within their salary range. Not one manager has been promoted into a vice presidency for over 12 years. In fact, eight vice presidents have been brought into NJU from the outside over the past eight years; there is a commonly held perception that the outside recruits have a very difficult time getting up to speed on how the organization works. The managers feel downtrodden and demoralized.

Lower level support staff were generally happy at NJU. They had a perceived sense of job security that they felt they have earned on the outside. As a result, they resisted several organizing attempts over the past several years.

There is a great deal of bitterness directed towards the Human Resources' people at NJU. They are insulated from both faculty and staff. Staff management has attempted to realign resources in their departments, when they first arrive at the University, but Human Resources has constantly blocked anything slightly resembling innovation. The HR Vice President, Al Smith, has mastered the art of answering a question by spending a four hour session picking apart the question, and, by his picking, suggesting that the questioner somehow is not fit psychologically for work at the University; such helpful intimidation has stanched the flow of questions arriving in his unit.

The hiring of new staff sends managers into convulsions. Literally, it takes twelve weeks to hire a new clerk. HR has grown a series of little Al Smith's who nit-pick every statement, job description, request for change, etc.. It is felt that candidates who make it through the search process are not the best available; they simply can tolerate the bureaucratic spin arounds. Hair on the back of the necks of staff management has been known to stand up just at the sight of Al Smith; he is frequently featured in their nightmares.

And Al is the individual responsible for the University's organizational design and resource alignment. He has worked years in preparing a pretty coherent sounding presentation upon how no change at NJU has been responsible for making it the great institution that it is; Al claims that NJU is the Harvard of the Meadowlands. Whenever a manager has questioned some of the premises of Al's arguments, that individual has received an outpouring of HR's helpful attention; perhaps not coincidentally, their affirmative action record has been scrutinized, their rate of worker's compensation claims being filed has been questioned, and the managers miraculously find themselves scheduled every three to four weeks for training sessions having to do with improving their interpersonal relations skills; Ed Fish over in Accounting ended up in one of the sessions having to feed peeled grapes to an Associate Provost while both were blindfolded and were required to sing, or at least listen to, Perry Como's most memorable love songs.

On top of this turmoil is the rumor that the budget ax is going to fall on NJU. Informed rumor has it that the budget for the next two fiscal years will be reduced by 9% each year. Enrollments are to be the same. There is not an opportunity for reducing the size of the 525 faculty members; their latest three year contract guarantees that no tenured or tenure-track faculty member can be laid off because of budgetary problems without one year's notice. Only 2% of faculty are candidates for lay-off. During the previous academic year, UPUNJ led its members on strike because of junior faculty having to share office space.

The President's Office has been working to address budgetary problems proactively. There have been several Presidential commissions over the years to analyze what NJU should do. He enlisted the support of six of the strongest and most well respected University leaders, from both the faculty and the key staffs, to study the issues. His team's recommendations were to do the following:

1. Develop a strong leadership statement from the top regarding what needed to be done. Identify the goals which individual deans/vice president's would be willing to buy into and articulate those goals clearly and accurately;
2. Reduce costs by 18% during the first 24 months of the process. The reduction would be $27 million on a base of $150 million.

You have been called as a member of a group into the President's Office. Upon entering, you are shocked at Dr. Vinson's state of anxiety. He charges you with coming up with a plan of action for him. One member of the team asks the President a minor question and he has an outburst of emotion; Vinson then apologizes. Your group understands that there is some urgency here.

President Vinson asks you to consider the following for preparation of your oral presentation for him:

1. Morale issues
2. Potential organizational issues
3. Realignment of the University's resources
4. Reward and recognition for facilitators of change
5. Compensation issues of the redesigned organization

6. Needed changes in the University's culture
7. Organizational barriers/enablers of change
8. Short term and long term strategies for change

Chapter 3

This Business of Culture: Reaction to Change

It is imperative that the facilitator of organizational change recognize that culture and all of its trappings have their origins in the biological world. Each of the components of culture had its origins when there were no cultures and no human beings. Regardless of all the noise and sophistication surrounding them, cultural values are evolutionary and are designed below levels of consciousness by men/women as biological organisms. It is their autonomic attempt at bringing into synchronization the external forces impacting the biological organism.

Though we pride ourselves upon our great technological accomplishments, which along several dimensions are great, and upon the incredible standards of living present within the United States and in other parts of the World, beneath the veneer of culture resides men and women who are forced to respond to the same kinds of biological stimuli as do the finch, the trout, and the grizzly bear. What obscures these facts is our enrollment into the concept that we who are fortunate enough to live in the present are really beyond all of that biological baggage that we believe sincerely to have vanished prior to our generation. As we will explore later, denial is a component of aversion to change and how we are constantly changing, both physiologically and intellectually.

Ironically, our satisfaction of biological needs has been convoluted in so many ways that we obscure their presence from our vision. Though it is incredibly easy for us to see biological activity in the animal world, we all too often fail to see it in our own. Suffice it to say that it is very much a part of our realities, whether it is acknowledged or not.

For instance, anyone who walks their dog understands that any other dog in their vicinity is more than willing to come over and check out the pooch. Clearly, these activities are rooted in biological needs. Rarely are these scent dances subtle; often times they are downright obnoxious. We occasionally accept the fact that a form of mating is going on in front of our eyes, but we don't focus upon it; we yank our dog's leash because we have things to do and people to see. Owners are reminded that their "best friends" who eat in the kitchen with them, play catch in their gameroom with them, and sometimes even sleep with them, can be pretty animal-like when they are around their peers.

In the business world, an appointment is made by the first time visitor to an executive for a particular time--10:00 a.m.. The individual arrives at the guard station or main receptionist desk at 9:45. The individual is asked to sign in; they are asked to wear a badge. They are told that it will be just a few moments. The guard calls up to a secretary who promptly at 10:00 a.m. comes down to meet the guest. Handshakes are exchanged and the guest is escorted to another waiting room. After fifteen minutes, the guest is ushered into the room of the host who has a retinue of four other people who will attend the meeting for some often times rather vague objectives.

If we analyzed the above scenario for just a few moments, utilizing the Primary Message System of Defense, it would become pretty clear that though our executives were not like the two dogs who appeared rather silly, they were participating in a defensive ritual to make sure that their biological organisms were okay. For instance, being greeted by the guards with guns strapped to their hips tends to intimidate most people; the guest is certainly sent the message that: "If there is trouble, we have the means to deal with it." Wearing a badge further humiliates the visitor, especially the ones that say: "Visitor--Escort Required," as in "you don't belong to this one big happy family." The secretary is another message sent to the visitor that "the boss is too busy with too may important things to come down and greet you; he will send an underling which is appropriate for your status." The retinue in the honcho's office suggests that this is really their meeting and that if there are any disputes, they certainly will be resolved in favor of the majority. In short, behind every action there is a biological root cause and it is critical that those causes be smoked out and analyzed to understand where the culture is going.

In addition, every reaction to a biological stimulus is a decision which has been made below levels of awareness and which is believed by the culture to be indisputable. Alternative possibilities are not fully articulated or entertained. The host at the meeting above may not have had any involvement in the elaborate defense mechanisms of which she is now a part but if push came to shove she would defend them as absolutely critical. Cultural norms and mores are rarely examined for their intelligence and utility. They are just there and become ratified because of the comfort they bring, not because they are the best way of satisfying the needs of the Primary Message Systems that will be discussed later.

For the organizational change process to be successful, change facilitators must take a proactive role in reflecting organizational culture back to those who are enmeshed in its fabric and who are unable to obtain a detached position of observation relative to it. Members of any culture are unable to identify with any kind of clarity the navigational paths through the barriers and enablers for the achievement of substantive change. They most certainly can identify broadstroke lines of force within their culture, but as the change process proceeds they become befuddled and angst-filled when asked to break through the many cultural barriers that block progress.

There are two non-examined beliefs that have currency among those who intervene into cultures and that have caused a great deal of mischief:

1) Many believe that culture is somehow magical and that if members of a culture are left to their own devices then everything will move them towards a state of splendor;

2) Interventionists have a repertoire of solutions that pretty much fit the needs of a wide range of cultures in turmoil; it is felt that if the facilitator has had experience within one utility culture, then that should fit another

utility. There is a sense that this cultural business is really pretty easy stuff and if you facilitated change easily in one   place, then it most certainly is transferable to another.

Anthropological research focuses upon the sanctity of each set of systems or beliefs of a culture. By working in cultures throughout the years, anthropologists have been able to provide all of us with a robust database of how cultures react within each of the ten Primary Message Systems so that we can obtain insight into the complexity and diversity of cultural reactions to similar phenomena. For instance, we know that women in Latin American Culture in the 1970's played a very different role in the education of their children than East Coast Women in the United States did during the same time, as well as playing a very different role in their children's education than do their daughters today.

None of this is to suggest that anthropologists believe that just because a culture does something in a certain way means that the culture is destined towards success or happiness for its members. Most anthropologists focus upon how cultures give meaning and have clearly identified how some cultures do just the opposite. Anthropologists who have worked for the federal government in an attempt to assist cultures thrive and survive repeatedly have found that the bureaucratic structure, and the bureaucratic cultures that accompany them, not only are not supportive of the bureau's attempt at achieving their goals but they also tend to create employees with incredibly high levels of cynicism; low morale is significantly more prevalent than in the worst private sector organizations.

In short, culture most certainly can support bringing out the best in the individuals who reside within it, as well as bringing out the worst. Individuals can blossom and flower because of their own drives without the nurturing support of culture, recognizing that in most instances such flowering will manifest itself in a relatively culturally accepted fashion. At its worse, culture can support and promulgate the maniacal visions of an Adolph Hitler and feel that while they were doing so all was well with the world.

Cultures can serve as a context for individual greatness to be nurtured and developed. It can bring forth eruptions of creativity such as that brought forth in Elizabethan England where any one of the three greats-- Marlowe, Jonson, and Shakespeare--each alone would have been the greatest literary genius of all time; they all three were contemporaries.

Culture can also drive or support a culture's movement towards its own destruction as evidenced in the downfall of the Soviet Union, the destruction of the Balkans, and the inhumanity present in the dictator state of Iraq. Erich Fromm states it most eloquently by looking at culture as a launch pad for self-actualization and meaning on the part of the individual:

> As long as man remains rooted incestuously in nature, mother, clan, he is blocked from developing his individuality, his reason; he remains the helpless prey of nature, and yet he can never feel one with her. Only if he develops his reason and his love, if he can experience the natural and the social world in a human way, can he feel at home, secure in himself, and the master of his life. It is hardly necessary to point out that of two possible forms of transcendence, destructiveness is conducive to suffering, creativeness to happiness. . . . It can be said that the concept of mental health follows from the very conditions of human existence, and it is the same for man in all ages and all cultures. Mental health is characterized by the ability to love and to create, by the emergence from incestuous ties to clan and soil, by a sense of identity based on one's experience of self as the subject and agent of one's powers, by the grasp of reality inside and outside of ourselves, that is, by the development of objectivity and reason. (Fromm, 1955, 68.)

Interventionists who feel that one or two successful interventions can serve as the model for a vast array of organizations and cultures fall into the mental trap of operating simplistically--a model that almost always fails. Cultures are so incredibly complex that the best thing the interventionist can do to achieve success is to develop a set of tools that will allow them to come up with viable models for the detection of lines of force within a culture. It can be argued validly that our interventions should be made with a panoply of models designed to sift out the true from the untrue.

The following example demonstrates how open eyes, open mind, and a focus upon data allow models to evolve from one culture; these models can be compared and contrasted with models derived from hundreds of cultures to be used in defining the lines of force within the culture and what the possible synthesized models might be for working through change in an organization.

The writer had the good fortune to be an active participant in the culture of Medellin, Colombia during the mid-seventies. Medellin was originally settled by Sephardic Jews, among others, who were fleeing the Inquisition in the 16th Century Spain. It had grown into the industrial center of Colombia with a particular focus upon the manufacturing of textiles; at one time it was the major, worldwide manufacturer of denim for Lee and Levi blue-jeans. During the mid-seventies, Medellin began a transition from a highly contexted culture where individuals knew who they were and what their aspirations should be to a culture where its entire foundation was shaken by the introduction of a new, no context group of *narcotraficantes*.

The members of the culture went through the following reaction to the change stimuli that bombarded them:

Cultural Reaction to Change: Medellin

* **Obliviousness** Medelli

* **Denial**

* **Self-deception**

* **Narcoses**

Initially, members of the culture were oblivious to what was happening. Violence increased, property changed hands more rapidly than at any other time in its history, the upper-class that had been the leadership backbone for centuries suffered a loss of power, but cultural blinders prevented the mass majority of people from noticing the changes. It is critical to keep in mind that we cannot see things which do not fit into our perceptual frames; if we have believed in a set of values and ways of operating in culture for years, it is going to take substantive and painful adjustments to see our world through different lenses than those to which we have become accustomed.

The phenomenon is similar to a lecture that occurred at Northwestern University during the streaking craze in the early seventies; a nude male--except for tennis shoes--walked from the top of the lecture hall to the bottom. The 100 plus students did not even focus upon this naked person. Finally when they did, they were frozen from acting. No one knew what to do. Finally, a woman in the front row started yelling at him that she was not paying the kind of money she was paying for tuition to have her lecture interrupted. She ordered him to get out of the room. He complied.

In Medellin, once the blinders allowed the change to become visible, there was a denial of its significance. The often heard reaction to change: "This too will pass," could be heard at family gatherings and social functions. Because most of the people in Medellin had only experienced how life had been lived for decades, they would not admit that anything would disrupt their lives and the way things had been.

The self deception stage tells the perceiver that though the changes are there, they really are of no significance. For example, several informants from the old upper class informed me that the drug traffickers brought new shopping malls, new apartment buildings, housing for the poor and a new standard of living; they let me know that things were much better off than they were before and that danger wasn't something foremost in their minds. On the day after one of the informants told me how much better things were, she was caught in a cross-fire of submachine guns while shopping for a new dress. Fortunately, she was not hurt; she convinced herself that the act was an anomaly and could never happen again.

When the change keeps rearing its ugly head on such a regular basis that members of culture can no longer self-deceive, they go into a state of narcosis. People numb themselves out because the change is too much for them to assimilate; when we are loaded up with Novocain in the dentist's chair, most of us feign sleep or boredom. We are not at our perceptual best. When outrageous things happen to our culture, we tend to numb out and our consciousness is directed away from the onslaught of new stimuli.

Sister Josephine and Narcoses

A very unfortunate incident is illustrative of the point. In the third grade, my teacher was a nun named Sister Josephine. She was not popular with any of the students in our class. We all knew that she was very sick and we suspected that she probably somehow deserved her pain.

One day my class members were reciting in class with Sister at the chalkboard, and as I looked up I saw the nun drawing a diagonal line from left to right that stopped in the chalk tray where her hand bounced off it and she fell to the floor. The similarities to the demise of the Wicked Witch of the West were amazing; however, no water was involved.

As I have worked with various groups of adults throughout the country, I have asked them what they believed the children did with the deceased nun in the front of the room. Rarely do they describe what happened.

Our class members did nothing in acknowledgment of the death. They numbed out because it was just too much. Sister passed away at 12:30 and we continued reciting our lessons until 2:30. In a bizarre twist, when our classmates were reciting, individuals nervously imitated Sister correcting them. No one went for help or cried. It is quite possible that some kids felt as if they brought this on through their silent, evil thoughts regarding the individual. We all went home and had a new teacher the next day; no one ever explained what had gone on; none of our students would use the *deathboard* where Sister had departed.

It is an often held belief that cultures are innately good and that they have evolved for some very sane reasons. It is argued that no one from the outside should really come into a culture and make evaluative statements regarding it when they cannot possibly understand all of the complex reasons why a culture is the way it is. This premise needs to be questioned on a continuing basis by the facilitators of cultural change because it is myopic by the culture who articulates it and it introduces that culture to the various landmines that are seeded by individuals who search for simplicity.

Both facilitators of cultural change and the members of the culture who are targeted for change suffer from the same class of myopia. The members of culture usually believe that where they are is just fine, with, perhaps, the need to tweak one or two things that will make life close to ideal. The change facilitators come in and they jump at attacking one or two problems that, with little surprise, are the one or two things they attacked at the previous engagement. Both mindsets are not only wrong, but they are destructive to both the culture and to the cultural interventionist.

In recent years, a growing body of study has developed which suggests that one of our greatest traps as human beings is to look at the world from a superficial, single faceted perspective. For the first 80 years of this century, it was entirely possible to decompose phenomena in the external world to make sense of them. Fragmentation was a way for folks to get their arms around tasks and to accomplish them successfully.

Examples of this include the powerful legacy which Frederick Taylor gave us with the slicing and dicing up of jobs. In manufacturing industries, initially, jobs were made so narrow that any able bodied man or woman from the street could learn relatively simple tasks and could repeat them for the rest of their lives. They could become productive very rapidly. His approach was then transferred to service industries because it was embraced widely as a model; within universities, industrial engineering departments honed the techniques until the system could be applied to a broad range of enterprises. The difficulty with the system was that the folks on the line had no idea about how their piece of work fit into the whole, what the person in front of them and behind them did, or why it was necessary for them to check their brain in at the door. They were not required to grow intellectually and though the money they earned was nice, their disembodiment from their work has resulted in outrageously high absenteeism rates, repetitive motion injuries, and substance abuse.

Within the service sector, one can observe this phenomenon repeatedly. When individuals in the information systems business attempt to migrate from legacy to distributed computing systems, they assume that the same organizational systems for the past will work in the future. They are attuned culturally to the fact that there are very few ways of doing things and what has worked in the past will work in the future. The bad news is that once change occurs the intellectual floodgates have to be opened so that the best options can be selected from the roaring stream of alternatives.

We race into the future, looking through the rear-view mirror."

Marshall McLuhan

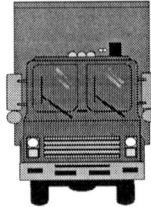

The client culture needs to be assisted by the interventionist with the exploration of options. Those options must consist of an understanding of all those beliefs consciously held by the majority of members of the cultures, as well as those unarticulated beliefs held by members that lie outside of consciousness. Fundamental success within any intervention is tied directly to the ability of the interventionist to totally reflect culture back to its members--from multi-faceted perspectives. Once they understand their beliefs when reflected back to them by an outside observer, they can then establish a foundation for change.

Michelangelo's *David*

During a recent trip to Florence, Italy, I went to a museum to observe Michelangelo's masterpiece *David*. As the tourist walks towards the hall that houses the masterpiece, one observes chunks of marble with parts of bodies emerging from them--an arm or two here, the start of a head here, shoulders, and so forth. A bit of research reveals that each of these marble chunks was a *David* that failed to emerge. Michelangelo would work and become frustrated with what was emerging, quit on that rock and move onto another.

Michelangelo believed that his job was to look at a piece of marble and envision what was within it. He would start chipping away with his chisel in an attempt to free the spirit from within the stone. His final *David* is a perfect example of freeing such a spirit.

Michelangelo's metaphor is strikingly relevant to what we need to do as change interventionists. We have to go into the change environment with the understanding that nearly everyone in the organization has a handle on what the organizational problems are; most of the folks on the lowest rungs of the pecking order know where the problems lie and, usually, they have known about them for quite some time. What folks are not good at is articulating the problems coherently and then laying out a plan of action for their solution. They usually carry a great deal of emotional baggage about the problems and they simply are not articulate about what needs to be done.

Per Michelangelo, our job is to chunk away at eliminating each and every one of the barriers necessary to achieve optimal unit performance, which includes a wide range of positive rewards for the folks who transform the organization. We need to let their collective spirit evolve and show them alternatives to being encased in their marble prisons. To do that, we must slowly expose pieces of culture and prepare everyone for the recognition that some pieces will need to be modified or removed and to work in preparation for the transition.

All concerned parties involved in this organizational transformation--whether facilitators of it or those who are cultural members whose culture will be transformed-- must be provided with the tools necessary to see the world from different vantage points and to see a multitude of options available to them. M. Mitchell Waldrop describes agents, or units of matter and behavior, configuring into complete entities:

> . . . agents were constantly organizing and reorganizing themselves into larger structures through the clash of mutual accommodation and mutual rivalry. Thus, molecules
> would form cells, neurons would form brains, species
> would form ecosystems, consumers and corporations would form economies, and so on. . . . Complexity, in other words, was really a sign of emergence. (Waldrop, 1992, 88)

Translated into organizational interventions, agents are those lowest level components which when added together form sets and eventually move into patterns. To the contrary of Mr. Waldrop's observations of the animal world, almost all organizations have moved towards compartmentalization--the slicing and dicing of functions into ever smaller and more controllable entities--which allows for the building up of specific turfs which evolve to a point of focusing upon internal rather than external customers. Entry into the environment will make clear that thousands and thousands of isolates--individual units of fragmentation--need to be joined together in some way or fashion so that they can be reconstituted into a larger whole.

The Disconnected Isolates

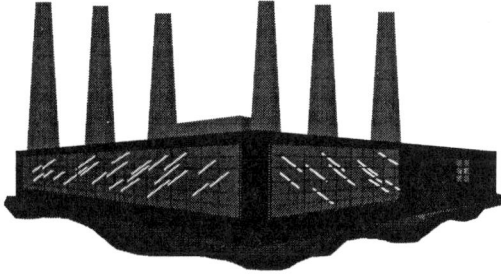

Priority Mail

In the early nineties, the U.S. Postal Service's marketing function decided that it was time to take on the likes of UPS and Federal Express by starting up a campaign to deliver any item under two pounds, in two days for $2.80. They advertised this service during the Olympics and large volumes of folks jumped on their bandwagon.

While I was working in a Postal Service's General Mail Facility in New York, I walked over to a hamper and observed it half full with magazines and other low priority non-letter mail and half-full with Priority Mail packages. I asked a supervisor to come over and explain what was going on. He explained that the marketing people kicked off this gigantic program without ever consulting the people who deliver the mail regarding whether it could be delivered. I asked the supervisor if it could be delivered within two days and he indicated that sure it could if its destination was New York. I asked whether it could be delivered as fast if its destination was Los Angeles. He indicated that sure but that it would probably take ten days--the same delivery time as that of the magazines.

Whereas the Postal Service is structured along a stovepipe design, each of the smokestacks does their own thing and rarely is there cooperation among the other stovepipes. In the case above, marketing had a hot idea and wanted to demonstrate how creative they were. They failed to work to any significant degree with mail processing to see if it was doable and how their capabilities could be worked into the design. As a result, the program was a failure, more Postal credibility was lost, and their percentage of delivery marketshare continues to drop. To date Postal has totally failed in moving their culture to one that is integrated; the situation is so serious that rarely do organizational change specialists even consider taking on the mother of all smokestacks.

"Complex, adaptive cultures are characterized by perpetual novelty."

At the time of intervention, we want to free up all of those agents who can join together in new configurations to move the organization forward. If one views a typical organization as an array of balls floating at random on a body of water, floating wherever various forces cause them to float, we can see the reactive nature of the organization; these balls represent the response heard all too often: "We've always done it that way." Under the new structural goal, these various components will be loosely bound together by a vision and a meaning for their existence that will allow them to explore the new and reconfigure in pursuit of it. They will find it in their best interest to quit all the wandering. We want to gently facilitate moving them in a direction that they viscerally believe is right but in which the organization has not encouraged them to move. Our job is to make all cultural members explorers of what can be, based upon the values of what has been.,

> . . . It was a two room adobe to which someone had connected a wooden frame lean-to with a roof of red composition shingles. A 1962 Chevrolet Impala squatted on cinderblock supports in the front yard, all four of its wheels missing. Chee pulled his patrol car to a stop beside it and sat waiting. If someone was home, willing to receive a visitor, he would appear at the door. If he didn't after a polite interval of waiting, Chee would knock. (Hillerman,   1980, 86-7)

For the change process to be successful, change facilitators must take a proactive role in reflecting organizational culture back to those who are enmeshed in its fabric but, as in the Hillerman example above, be respectful towards the privacy and space needs of members of the culture. Members of any culture are unable to identify with any kind of clarity the navigational paths through the barriers for the achievement of substantive change. They most certainly can identify broadstroke lines of force within their culture, but as the change process proceeds they become befuddled and angst-filled when asked to break through the many cultural barriers that block progress

Alfred Korzybski, the inventor of General Semantics, once wrote: "Avoid evaluation until comprehension is complete." By that he meant that the interjection of judgment by the investigator of the communication patterns within cultures results in the development of blindspots that will negatively impact their future work.

The Change Cycle

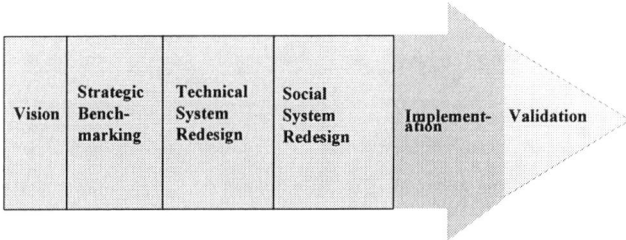

Vision	Strategic Bench-marking	Technical System Redesign	Social System Redesign	Implement-ation	Validation

One tool that has been very useful is the above change cycle model. In using it, an organization can be led systemically to perpetual change. When this model is coupled with prior models that we will examine, a powerful tool kit is available to the interventionist. Its key components are:

Vision

In every culture, we have individuals who are able to think out of the box to such an extent that we listen to them; mind you, that outside of the box cannot go too far or people do not listen. However, these folks serve the purpose of letting the dominant culture think beyond what they were previously capable without horribly offending them. Examples of these shamans, priests, or oracles   might   include: Pope John Paul II,   Nelson Mandela,and Jean Kirpatrick.

At the client site, we want to define what the current patterns of thinking are and radically change them using this visioning process. We want to respectfully challenge each and every pattern possible without alienating the cultural members. If you buy the premise that   the spirits of these   folks   are trying to get out of the dense rock that confines them,   objective question making can support such an evolution.

Strategic Benchmarking

Once the visioning has been completed, we can be assured that the cultural artifacts that came out of that experience are significant but are not out of the box. The conservativism of all culture almost guarantees that first pass work will reflect only token elements of change.   We then must move onto strategic benchmarking   that will force our clients into a different way of looking at the world-- beyond tokenism.

One way of viewing this activity is paralleling that which anthropologists have studied and documented for years--one tribe moves into an area and begins introducing its technologies, norms, and mores to others. The common result is that the original inhabitants learn very different ways of being than those which they held sacrosanct originally. The original culture very might well learn that its culture has hidden many more of its beliefs and ways of being than what it originally thought possible. (Of course, if the new culture's values and beliefs are too far out from their beliefs, reactions can range from mild discomfort to the waging of war).

The interventionist wants to accomplish the same sort of cultural value testing opportunity for their client. If an organization is a business, why shouldn't it look at every one of the operational systems of the best in the business to show the profundity of difference? Today, a multitude of companies and their systems are documented in databases which can be accessed relatively inexpensively and the inputs drive the culture to become first in class. The organization realizes that it is not going to get to where it wants to get using the same old systems that it has used in the past.

Technical System Redesign

In order for the interventionist to affect change across the enterprise, there must be a decomposition of all of the enterprise's technical processes. These might include what steps are executed to buy a horse, to cut a payroll check, or to be promoted. These processes start with a customer's needs and move horizontally across to the satisfaction of the customer.

The redesign has to do with modifying the chain of value from the customer's perspective so that all of the new vision and data obtained from the strategic benchmarking can be incorporated into it. In orders of magnitude the new stream should be approximately 50% more valuable than the previous one. For instance, when the Postal Procurement Value Stream was redesigned, cycle time was reduced from 62 to 2 days.

Social System Redesign

If the Technical Systems go horizontally from the customer, the Social Systems are those which move vertically down onto the value stream. Apart from the business organization they might include individuals designated to hand out Communion at Mass, designations of who is elected to homeowners committees, who is designated as a suitable mate for an upper-class individual in Colombian   society, and who can play the character of Christ for Easter ceremonies. Within organizations, they include, but are not limited to, work unit configuration, management feedback systems for employees, compensation systems, career ladders, etc.

There are organizational change characteristics of social system redesign that are very different from the technical system domain--it tends to be suffused with emotion and suspicion, lacks a great deal of benchmarking models to which it can be compared, and there is always a firm, non-articulated commitment by management to retard changes in it from happening. Many of my clients are willing to step up to the plate and   take on all sorts of technical changes but they do not feel comfortable messing with the social systems. Needless to say, the social systems are   the reinforcers for the other changes to be made; if you do not change them, you will never change anything substantive.

Implementation

It is convenient in models like these to place implementation towards the end of the change process in the belief that one does not need to worry about it until the end of the total process. In fact, it is critical that the change facilitator begin implementing small changes shortly after entry into the change environment. It is the only way to know what real change folks are ready for, opposed to the words which suggest that change is possible. Note: 95% of failures in change processes   occur   during implementation; that is why it is so critical to incorporate elements of implementation from the get go.

Validation

This process is simply the matter of establishing metrics to gauge whether you accomplished what you said you would and then testing whether you achieved them. Clearly, the results data need to be fed back into the design for changes during subsequent iterations.

The Stages of Group Development

Whenever the interventionist enters into an environment, they must assess where their organization is and through which phases they must pass.. Research and experience have demonstrated clearly that the group can only move as far as it is ready to move. The facilitator should use the following models in the toolkit to optimize change opportunities.

The Stages of Group Development

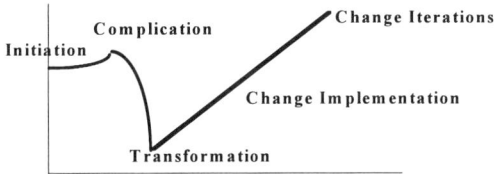

1. Initiation Phase--members of a change team arrange for the appropriate resources to be obtained to "transform" their culture. The group is highly committed to needed changes in their organization; in many cases, group members are selected because they "tell it like it is" regarding the inadequacies of the current organization. Though the group is often energized, supported by ample financial and human resources, and supported by all levels of the organization, they all wear, albeit subtly at times, cultural straitjackets which narrow their frames of reference for what is possible; they carry with them sub-conscious rules and hidden agendas which will manifest themselves obliquely during the next phase.

Work during this phase is congenial interpersonally and is quite enjoyable; outputs of this phase tend to be restricted to grandiose visions held by some team members which are unshared with others, or team generated changes which are superficial, or cosmetic modifications which often have to do with improving the creature comforts and visual appeal of plant and offices. During this stage, would-be leaders begin lining up support for their points of view; group members begin to evaluate how the group is functioning and each develops a subjectively based set of expectations that will rear their nasty heads during iterations in the next phase.

2. Complication Phase--just as the Initiation Phase was characterized by energy, enthusiasm, and vision, albeit fragmented, this phase is characterized by their counterpoints-- despair, frustration, and team member disorientation to what the goals of the process are. During this Phase, individual team members will withdraw, become verbally aggressive towards

others, demonstrate demoralization, and will seek opportunities for escaping the group. Irrational behavior will manifest itself; group productivity is low and often times centers upon developing detailed plans, collecting data, conducting studies, and reformulating reports. Organizational barriers are bemoaned, but no substantive plans are made to transform the organization; to the contrary, small picture activities are embraced as valuable since big picture issues seem insurmountable.

Phase 3--Transformational Synergy, Phase 4--Change Implementation, and Phase 5--Change Iterations are not entered into because of organizational barriers which the team encounters. Their lack of perspective prevents them from negotiating themselves around them. The group tends to fade away or pursues minor projects that allow them, and their executive sponsors, to organizationally save face.

Viable, thriving, non-business cultures develop systemic change mechanisms to enhance their survivability. They maintain the old but charge change agents with introducing the new into them. Thriving cultures do so because of the creative energies supplied by their scientists, philosophers, artists, religious and political, and social leaders. As indicated in Illustration 1, as the culture moves in the direction of peaking relative to its total livability/survivability, new cultural drivers kick in(the dotted line) to assure that Phase 2 peak performance can be achieved. The model is critical for analyzing the sustainability of excellence in business cultures as well as in general culture. It reveals the criticality for the change facilitator to provide guidance and change options to clients.

The Cultural Change Model

One way for the change practitioner to view organizational culture is as a protozoan type of organism. Study of the model will assist in the specification of change strategies for each culture as a uniquely configured organization. The model's utility is in its ability to represent how culture's react to change, as will be demonstrated in subsequent iterations.

The Stasis Model

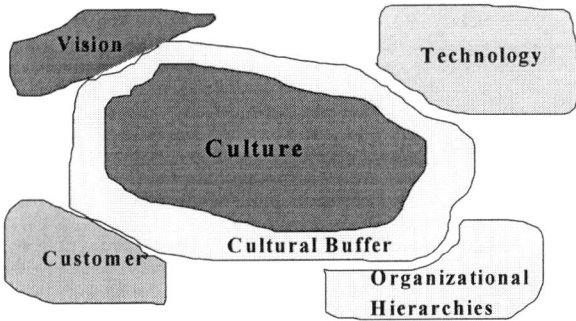

Its six components are:

Culture is composed of the total communication systems present within the culture; these systems contain its values and beliefs and the mechanisms for acculturating new members of the culture to the same.

Cultural Buffer Zone--

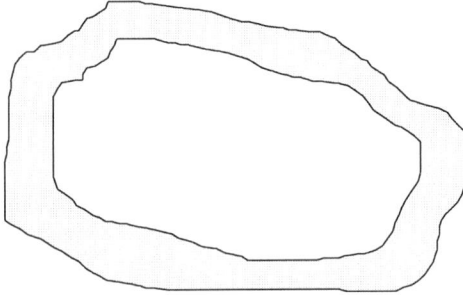

The Cultural Buffer Zone is the elastic barrier that reacts to external threats to cultural inertia by seeking out the threats, surrounding, and neutralizing them. The Zone is the cultural equivalent to the body's dispatch of antibodies when invaded by a foreign agent.

Change Agent: Technology

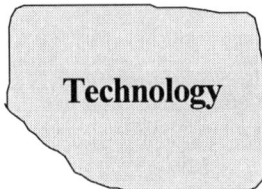

Technology

Based upon the work of McLuhan, technology is any extension of the mind, body, or senses. Cultures more readily embrace the agents of change as contained, and most often hidden, in technology than when change boldly knocks on a culture's door. When technologies resemble previous versions of the same, the culture is less likely to perceive it as an invasion of a foreign and noxious agent. For instance, a re-engineering effort aimed at updating a management information system can be embraced by the organization if bought into by all levels of the enterprise; such technology have served in the past as the Trojan Horse of cultural change--it will bring changes with it, but will not, in most instances, cause violent reactions in the culture.

Change Agent: Vision--

A strong vision articulated by a well-respected individual in the organization, and bought into by the total organization because the leader's credibility, can be seen as non-threatening by the culture. The visionary must be perceived as being a part of the culture and being committed to the people as integral parts of the change effort. For instance, Iacocca's leadership at Chrysler was seen in the above light; he was respected as an experienced and competent automotive expert who assumed significant professional risk by taking on the challenge. He also arranged a first--for Douglas Fraser, then President of the UAW, to sit on the board of a major U.S. corporation.

Change Agent: Organizational Hierarchies

A management team is perceived by the culture to play primarily a maintenance role. Most managers do spend most of their time protecting the status quo, rather than assisting in organizational transformation. When management breaks out of the role by reacting to substantive change, and thus changing their role as cultural maintainers, they are reacted to as external change agents and rejected by their organization. Within most change efforts, they are perceived as being barriers to change; the recent history of re-engineering efforts suggests that roles need to be defined for these managers by the executives and by the change facilitator for them to support change efforts and to be a critical, constructive part of the re-engineered organization.

Change Agent: Customers--

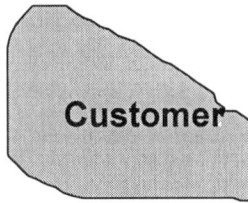

As are management, the influence of customers upon cultural change are ever present and are tolerated by the organization until such time as they threaten cultural inertia. Historically, cultures react to threatened markets by making significant investments in old technologies, i.e., Swiss watchmakers when challenged by non-analog technology, IBM's initial reactions to the personal computer threat, General Motor's initial reluctance to acknowledge Japanese manufacturing capabilities and its continuing failure to embrace re-engineered models created by Saturn Corp. etc..

Interactions of the Elements:

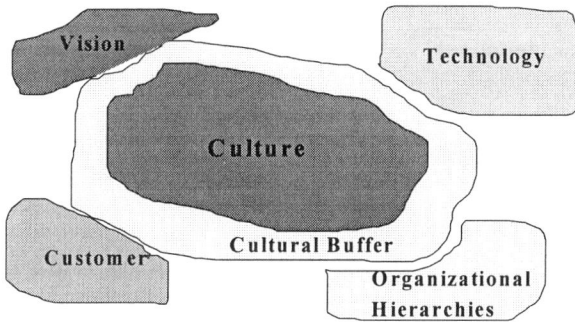

As indicated in the model above, the organization is in a state of relative inertia. The Cultural Core is protected from external change agents by the Cultural Buffer Zone; the four change agents live peripherally close to the culture but in most circumstances, do not threaten it, i.e., Technology, Vision, Management, and Customers.

The change facilitator's role primarily is to work with the organization in the change areas of technology and visioning. The objective is to move the organization towards outrageous future goals as defined in the vision and to explore technology options to support such change. For instance, the cultural state of equilibrium suggests the facilitation of an organizational vision which helps identify how re-engineered value streams will increase productivity and reduce costs by designing a less fragmented, redesigned organization to support customer to customer value-added business processes; to support such an organization, Information Engineering work needs to be completed to redistribute operational information via the appropriate technology. Most middle management will resist the potential realignment of information and power. Another significant challenge for the facilitator is the lack of urgency with which the organization proceeds because it does not see a threat; the change process might be so casual that the facilitator becomes engulfed into the culture and starts talking and behaving as if they were born into it.

The difficulty with the casual change process is that if an external threat does hit hard and fast, the facilitated change process might not be perceived as being quick enough to respond; past change performance speed might result in the perception that too little can be done fast enough to ward off the threat. In these circumstances, numerous organizations opt for a Slash and Bleed approach.

The S&B process, though vulgar sounding and organization-ally dysfunctional, achieves short term solutions to financial pressures; rapid change is executed swiftly and effortlessly. Unfortunately, it demoralizes employees and damages the organization's ability to meet effectively future change opportunities which face it; in addition, since the S&B process is a fragmented approach which seldom focuses upon systemic change, the initial cost savings and productivity improvements tend to evaporate as cultural inertia pulls the organization back to where it was prior to the reactive decision. If the consultant survives the S&B process, they are perceived as being part of management and lose the credibility necessary for future success.

Some enterprises have experienced the power of developing and nurturing learning cultures as a part of their way of doing business--cultures that reinforce the value of incorporating a continuous change methodology within them. When Roger Smith headed General Motors, he supported the development of the Saturn Corporation as a non-traditional GM culture which would serve as a model from which the mother culture could learn; organizational mechanisms and methodologies were put in place to transfer learning between the two cultures. Clearly, the challenge of the change interventionist is to facilitate ample learning and change for the organization to be perceived by management and board members as making steady and substantive progress but which is not seen by the culture as being so substantive as to trigger defense mechanisms in protection of the cultural

Cultural Reaction to One Change Event Model

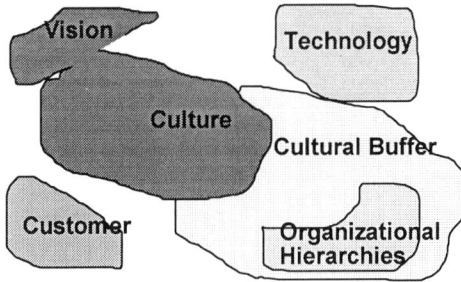

Interactions of the Elements

As indicated above, when the Cultural Core senses a threat from Change Event 1, it dispatches the Cultural Buffer Zone to attack and take out the threat. The Cultural Core becomes more vulnerable from the remaining four elements because of the reduced buffering. The organization focuses upon taking out the threat; if additional threats present themselves, the culture will numb itself to them until such time as the threat becomes overwhelming, and, perhaps, debilitating. Such a cultural configuration results in its being relatively reactive in its current state and until such time when it re-establishes equilibrium.

The change facilitator's role primarily is to work with the organization in using the crisis as an opportunity for developing a vision and using technology as vehicles for the introduction of systematic change. The organization is ripe for an alternative change process that is proactive in nature and relatively limited in scope. All four EE lenses can be used for the re-engineering of significant, but relatively restricted business activities.

The Cultural Reaction to Two Change Events Model

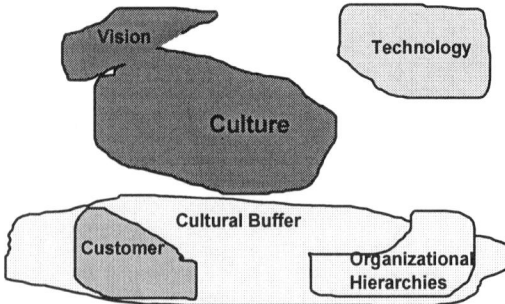

Interactions of the Elements:

With the additional change event attacking the culture when it is vulnerable, most cultures first numb themselves to the forces and become focused upon cultural maintenance and retreat. The cultural core retracts and begins shedding value systems. Chaos reigns within the organization but is not recognized for what it is. Morale is at an all-time low; employees are disoriented.

The change facilitator's role becomes one of assisting in developing a vision for identifying the current chaos and overcoming it, as well reinventing the organization. Opportunities for change are too many, participants are almost too willing to move, and the facilitator's challenge is focusing the energies into constructive directions. The facilitator takes on the role of old cultural system maintenance so that new cultural systems can be developed.

The Maintainable Cultural Change Model

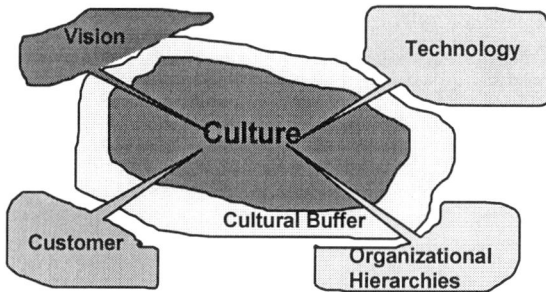

Interactions of the Elements:

All four of the Change Agents are actively interacting with the Core Culture; all are impacting it to varying degrees. The change facilitators focus should be upon growing the impact of the vision and technology change agents and reducing the impact of markets and management. Markets often serve as inhibitors to long-term visioning processes in the enterprise; clearly, market scans should be used to help build the vision and to assist in identifying technology needs. As previously discussed, management's influence tends to be reactive, rather than proactive, to change and therefore should be used as facilitators of growing the technology and vision change agents.

Summary

The change facilitator's primary responsibility is to understand the client culture and its current relationship to change processes and to use such knowledge in forging the establishment of a vision that sets outrageous goals for the organization. The facilitator assists the organization in re-engineering value streams, within the context of planning for future technology design. The facilitator's mission is to push the culture that prefers being inert into change modalities without triggering its change antibodies. Incremental improvement is then worked upon in previous phase change simultaneous to current phase change efforts.

The facilitator's primary responsibility is working the organization through the complication stage of its development so that substantive change can occur. Such movement rests upon their sensitivity to the organizational and interpersonal dynamics opaquely manifesting themselves, as well as working within the company for proper organizational alignment. The organization will always configure itself to get the results it wants; the change facilitator reflects back what the cultural values are currently and what they potentially could be in the future.

Chapter 4

Components of Infrastructure

Overview

Organizations are perfectly designed to get the results that they get. If the Skunkworks at Apple Computer during the reign of Steve Jobs developed the Macintosh, it was because the organizational infrastructure supported a series of breakthroughs that made the machine possible. The fact that Apple now is looking at some pretty uninspiring performance is certainly related to the absence of those underlying components that drive individuals and organizations to greatness. Recent layoffs, non-payment of bonuses, and systemic churning of their human resources pretty much make their performance in the early eighties ancient history.

Markets also clearly have an impact upon the performance of an organization. So does competition. Clearly, leadership plays a significant role. However, how is it that Apple stock was every stockholder's dream in the early '80s and it no longer is? And how is it that a Ford Motor Company, or a Saturn, or a Dell Computer who are all facing significant challenges similar to Apple's, have transformed themselves when Apple has not?

Throughout this volume, we have held to Hall's definition that: "Culture is communication; communication is culture." As a part of that definition is embedded the concept that every organizational structure that we create, every memo that we write, every compensation package that we put together, every arbitrary action that we make, and every time management and their subordinates act is an expression of cultural value. All of these things are expressions of a culture and they can be studied just as other cultural artifacts can be studied.

In fact, there is an entire school of anthropology that argues that we have to be very wary of what individuals tell us regarding what is happening in their culture. We can learn significantly more by analyzing cultural artifacts than by interviewing individuals. It is not that people knowingly misrepresent the truth, they simply communicate their tapes to us and there may be very little reference to phenomena in the verifiable world.

A Case Study: A Cultural Artifact

Recently, one of my colleagues and I were discussing the need for one of our federal clients to develop project management skills for their organization. Their unit was not doing particularly well and the head of the unit felt that what they needed was the discipline of project management. He told us to go and see what we could put together to meet his need.

As a part of our planning we focused upon the lack of discipline that characterized the way these folks went about their business. They would ignore their employees and their sub-contractors until a project was about due, and then they would descend upon them with all sorts of unreasonable requests, as well as with new definitions of what was due. The sub-contractors in particular would go into shock when this happened because they risked not receiving pay if the client was not satisfied with their work.

To conserve their energy, the sub-contractors did not work very hard until the sponsor defined what had to be done and then they worked sixteen hour days to meet the goal. The federal employees spent most of their time doing very little because the craziness was something that they were accustomed to so they simply numbed themselves to the irrationality because they had job security.

My colleague and I came up with a very comprehensive project management strategy that had been tested over a broad range of clients. We packaged the content of the strategy into a series of mini-courses that could be taken by the managers and supervisors at their convenience. We designed a structure for having pre-tests and post-tests available to the trainees so that those who already knew the material could show their proficiency and bypass the test.

The project was killed when we learned that even supervisors and managers in this organization could not be given tests on courses. They do not have to demonstrate proficiency and no information of any kind can be entered into their personnel folders if they refuse to take a test. It is a common practice for management to sleep through and not attend mandatory training for them (sic). There are no consequences for such behaviors.

How do these artifacts reveal values? As hypotheses, what other less obvious values might reside within similar structures to the above?

In general, components of today's infrastructures are incompatible with the values that organizations wish to reinforce. In the United States, there have been breakthroughs after breakthroughs in productivity across a wide range of industries, but many organizations remain unproductive by using the same work-unit structures that they have for sixty years because no one has taken the leadership to change them. Most companies are still organized hierarchically in departments when research has demonstrated that companies can eliminate 40% of their cost and bottlenecks by designing their organizations cross-functionally. Management continues to pay itself bonuses for improvements in the performance of the organization, but an incredible number of firms believe that hourly employees would not be motivated with similar incentives as those paid to executives.

Experience has demonstrated that if the executive sponsors of a project are not interested in the change team's modification of any or all of the components of infrastructure, they are not ready for the change process to begin. It is recommended that if they are not willing to open all of these items up to exploration, with the understanding that the team must come up with financially responsible recommendations, it is preferable to kill the project then than to spend a great deal of resources on an activity that cannot succeed. It is critical that if we are to change culture we be able to change it complexly with the buy-in of the whole organization, not in a piece-meal fashion that will satisfy only a small slice of the company.

Below are each of the components of infrastructure that are critical in supporting both the cultural and individual change that we discussed in the previous chapters. In the culture of the United States, we have not invested the kind of organizational change talent to custom design each of the components within companies. We have spent enormous amounts of resources on the technical processes of the organization but have not paralleled such investments there with those in the social arena. The following discussions should provide the reader with a framework for so doing.

1. Skill Decomposition

If we analyze a culture's documentation of skills that it says are needed to do jobs relative to what in fact skills are present within the culture, we inevitably discover significant disconnects. Skills needed to accomplish work are organic and most organizations spend insufficient time in tracking how such processes occur. Most organizations rely upon the individuals doing the work to identify what they are doing, to write their own job descriptions, and to be the drivers behind what skills evolve for a given job. Therefore, it clearly is not accidental how the skills required for the job remain static over time and how innovation in social areas generally is non-existent.

This lack of sophistication in documenting skills and working to systemically move the skills into evolving results in a skill narcissism that cripples the evolving organization. The narcissism manifests itself when an individual who has evolved skills, is relatively successful at executing them, and as a respected part of the culture is requested to develop a newspaper ad to hire additional individuals or to evaluate other individuals within the same, or similar, positions. The individual, regardless of their level in the organization, gravitates towards seeking out someone just like them. The net result is the homogeneity so characteristic of some organizations that it significantly stifles the introduction of new into the culture which results in organizational stagnation.

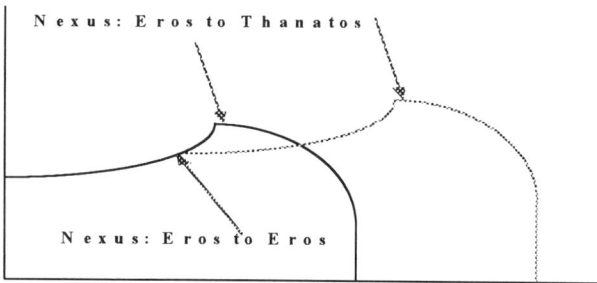

This very same phenomenon in the skills area reflects the same model of how organizational culture, and organizations, die. On the far left side of the chart above, at birth organizations, as are very young children, are filled with life and despite start-up obstacles they grow and prosper. The first arrow at the top represents the plateauing of an organization or a brief point of stasis. If the organizational culture was visionary enough to see the need for an infusion of the new into it, it would have done so prior to the old culture peaking. The net result would be that one organizational component that thrived and then outgrew its usefulness is replaced by a totally new component.

This model illustrates the need in all cultures for there to be a renewal factor built within it. Cultures must be challenged with stimuli that keep it fresh and alive. Marriages that are happy are those where both partners go out of their way to keep the relationship fresh. On the same hand, organizations must constantly build up the skill sets of their employees or vitality disappears.

Inventories of employee skill sets are relatively easy to extract. The investigator very simply decomposes activities executed by employees by asking them. Once these decompositions are done for an entire enterprise, one can work with employees to see how reconfigurations of who does what can bring greater productivity and greater satisfaction for all employees.

2. Behavioral Maps

Intuition would tell us that if culture restricts the development of complex skills within positions that there would be, in all likelihood, a restriction · upon the development of complex behaviors in these same individuals. While consulting in Washington D.C. to various federal clients during the first two years of the Clinton administration, it was said by various groups of clients that: "Things were not going well at the White House, but that pretty soon Clinton was going to bring in the grownups to make things happen." Unless specific designs are made that systematically develop complex behavioral skills within an organization, the behavioral map will be one dimensional.

Below are examples of activities to be performed with their corresponding behaviors. Code keys are at the bottom of the page.

Procurement ReEngineering: Partial Behavioral Map for the Redesigned Activities

1) DEFINE REQUIREMENT/NEED

- AV   Assign unique number for tracking purposes
- AV   Assign to specific BC
- HAV   Define & Write SOW, specifications, and level of evaluation criteria needed
-   H   Identify level of administrative responsibilities desired in contract
- HA   Prepare cost estimate
-   H   Identify & Develop various basic and unique requirement needs/description
- HA   Develop acquisition strategy and feedback mechanisms(milestones, etc..)
-   A   Request and obtain DOL wage determinations
-   A   Prepare in-house contract file

(2) DEVELOP SOURCE OPTIONS

- AV   Determine source availability (include customers local area)
- A   Search for SMWBE source opportunities
- AV   Determine if available from excess
- AV   Search for previous acquisitions for same or similar items
- AV   Determine if available from other agencies contracts
- HV   Determine marketplace
- AV   Advertise as appropriate (e.g., COM, Business Daily, local areas)
- A   Obtain source evaluations (prequalification opportunities)
- HA   Single source document?
- A   Complete source list

(3) PR APPROVAL

- A   Finalized PR generated and approved (includes budget debit)
- A   Acknowledgment and finalized acquisition strategy

H=Human Activities Performed
A=Administrative Activities Performed
V=Value Added

In addition, a wide range of other behavior descriptors can be used to characterize them. What knowledge is required? Are the behaviors of an interpersonal nature? Are the behaviors conducive to full participation in team activities? etc..

3. Job Definition

Once the activities, skills and behaviors present within an organization have been identified, jobs can be designed into new configurations. Skilled facilitation of knowledgeable employees who represent a cross section of the organization can accomplish such tasks in a relatively short period of time.

More likely than not, the new designs will result in job configurations significantly different from previously. It is critical to note that just as we have relied upon the critical relationships between 1. Skill Decomposition, Behavioral Maps, and Job Definition to intelligently design the new jobs, we must also reinforce desired behaviors with modified systems for: 4. Compensation, 5. Organizational Acculturation, 6. Recruitment, 7. Career Progression, 8. Development, 9. Feedback Mechanisms, and 10. Non-Compensation Drivers. All of these are required to work together to consciously achieve the desired organizational goals.

The Saturn Corporation, and others, have provided job definition models that we can view for comparison and contrast to our own. In most cases, it is easy to observe how relatively hidebound we have become relative to the creativity that we use in designing new jobs. Whereas our businesses have changed radically, our job structures have remained the same.

Below is a synthesis of new structures that require that each employee be responsible for each of the following items, in addition to their specific technical expertise:

Principles

1. Self-managed work teams who are paid for team productivity are the   most productive.
2. Self-management of the team will replace traditionally managed teams and rotation of management roles will occur for the various team members.
3. The self-managed team will meet or exceed all of the productivity goals and standards of traditional organizations given the same volume of work as a minima; incentive rewards will be established to reinforce behaviors that will result in 1.5x+ productivity goals and standards of traditional similar organizations.

Each self-managed team member will:

1. Reach decisions by consensus
2. Make their own job assignments
3. Be self directed
4. Resolve their own conflicts
5. Plan their own work
6. Design their own jobs
7. Control their own workflows, materials and inventory
8. Schedule their own communication within and outside of groups
9. Keep their own work unit records
10. Make selection decisions of new members into the group
11. Constantly seek improvements in quality, cost and the work environment
12. Integrate horizontally with business team resources
13. Perform to their own budget
14. Facilitate group growth into higher productivity
15. Determine their own methods of work
16. Schedule their own vacations/time off/substitutes
17. Maintain/perform their own health and safety maintenance programs.
18. Be responsible for producing quality products to schedule at competitive costs
19. Assist in developing and delivering their own training
20 Seek resources as needed
21. Schedule and hold their own meetings
22. Initiate the initial consultative procedure for self-corrective action with individual level responsibility

4. Compensation

The Parable of the Perseverant Consultant

Phil Schwartz was considered by many to be the best organizational change consultant in the business. He had worked for fifteen years in the business and if someone really had difficulties, they came to him. Phil's approach was to think complexly about problems and then solutions would bubble up to the surface.

Phil was tasked by a very high executive in one of the largest governmental agencies to introduce a new compensation plan that would improve significantly employees' productivity. Phil traveled the country until he found the unit with who he wished to work in developing the system. It was located in the Southwest and of all the units in the organization, he knew that it would work.

Phil worked through unit management and obtained their commitment to try something new; the management was open to innovation and they were being clobbered by Headquarters because of their relatively astronomical labor costs. Phil interviewed most of the key stakeholders in the unit including organized labor and a cross-section of the levels of the organization. He made friends and was ready for his first Core Team meeting with those fourteen people whom best represented the sentiment of the other 1500 people in the unit. Core Team members included four management folks, two members of union leadership, and all other layers of the work force.

On the first meeting, Phil walked in tall and proud and ready to knock off a big win. He engaged in various warm and fuzzy kind of warm up exercises and then popped the question, the answer to which would make him smile: "What would we need to do to reduce costs here by 10%?" The Core Team's eyes glazed over. Their mouths hung agape. Minutes passed before one person said: "Phil, I guess I thought you understood what is going on here. We have given and given and given to Headquarters and there no longer is anything to give. We cannot cut costs by 10% of 1%. Now do you understand?" Bobbing heads filled the room and Phil's *huevos rancheros* began to threaten revolt. He misjudged seriously, completed non-threatening activities for the rest of the session, and raced onto the nearest plane to Washington.

Phil returned two weeks later and worked with each of the Team members in preparation for the next session. He could not believe his ears. They continued with their story that a dime was not to be cut. Despite his skill and intelligence, he asked the same 10% question as before and was greeted with the same response. He again regretted having eaten breakfast, conducted the session, and hightailed it back to Washington.

Two weeks later Phil was flying back to the unit from National Airport and he reviewed what looked to be a trail of disasters on his road to his first failure. He tossed and turned in his seat, unable to enjoy the in-flight movie entitled, *Father of the Bride.* As he was going out of his way to be distracted from his pressing professional problems, one of the scenes caught his attention. Steve Martin's character refused to pay money for the very exquisite wedding trappings provided by some kind of a wedding artist from somewhere in the ex-Eastern Bloc. Phil watched and it all came together for him--Steve was not interested in doing something if there was no reward in it for him. His spouse and daughter might enjoy the frivolities, but he would much rather enforce his value of frugality than go along with theirs. Phil pondered that it was entirely possible that he wanted reduced costs in the unit, and so did the management, but why shouldn't the workers be as stingy as can be since they got nothing for it?

Phil was good and knew it but he was uncertain. He was so uncertain that he ate four chalky antacid tablets for breakfast. He walked into the session. He popped the same 10% question and got the same response as twice before. Rather than letting the tension continue, he hit the group with a new question:

"I understand that you don't feel that anything can be saved, but let's look at the problems in a new way. This unit spends $355 million a year on wage and materials to conduct our various processes. What would happen if you could cut $36 million in costs during the first year? Then what would happen if we returned $24 million in savings to the taxpayers during the second year, and we paid out the remaining $12 million to all 1500 employees in the plant equally over a two year period of time? Do you think you could cut the costs?"

There was uniform agreement. Everyone in the group felt that a 20% cut was possible. There was some mumbling about such a scenario never being approved by management, though high-level managers were on the team who approved the scenario.

Compensation has long been used as a tool by management to control their subordinates. It has been used to reinforce outrageously conformist behavior and to discourage thinking or acting in a fashion that threatens their narrowly defined *status quo*. Compensation determinations have been delegated most often to human resource and accounting personnel, both functions characterized most often as being significantly distanced from the business that makes the enterprise viable.

There are any number of options available to the change management team to move towards a more equitable payment of employees for manifesting desirable behavior. There are strong trends occurring currently to make employees' pay directly related to their productivity. The absolute key to dealing intelligently with these very difficult pay issues is to work within the culture to make sure that management is not the only cultural voice to be heard in this area.

Below is a model of how many innovative companies are structuring pay. It is a synthesis of several cutting edge organizations who have formed employee committees to work in the design of the system.

Major Manufacturer's Infrastructure: An Alternative Compensation Modely

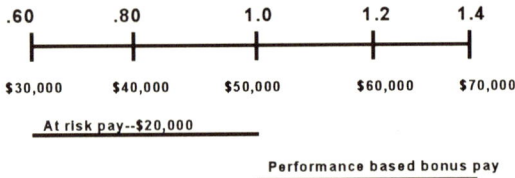

.60	.80	1.0	1.2	1.4
$30,000	$40,000	$50,000	$60,000	$70,000

At risk pay--$20,000

Performance based bonus pay

The 1.0 on the scale represents an employees mid-point in a range starting at .6 and moving to 1.4. Based upon this system, an employee knows at their date of hire that they can earn anywhere from $30,000 to $70,000 a year.

Our theoretical employee is at the mid-point in his range and is slotted to make $50,000 a year. The system as it is articulated up to now lets the employee know that he is entitled to that pay and whether he really hustles or sleeps is not factored into the formula.

What employees are doing, is saying: "Wait a minute. My value is that I am willing to work hard. I want to send my kids to college and I am fed up carrying some of the deadbeats around this place. I will take some risk if I know that management will play with me fairly." They then are putting up to forty percent of their mid-range pay at risk, knowing that they will perform to the agreed upon performance standards. Furthermore, these folks have negotiated that if they exceed their goals and then some, they are entitled to a forty percent bonus over the mid-point, in addition to company bonus payouts.

We can not spend significant time discussing the multitude of compensation models that there are out there. Suffice it to say that if employees know what the goals are, and there is an infrastructure for total quality, continuous learning, and mutual trust within the environment, systems can be designed with cross-functional teams to assist the enterprise in moving in life sustaining directions.

One month ago, I took a colleague of mine from South America to the Saturn Plant outside Nashville. Wherever the trolley traveled out in the manufacturing facility, employees would keep working but smile, wave, and yell their greetings to us. My friend asked me if I believed they were sincere. I said I was not sure. He told me that what was fantastic about the experience was that in his plant, they could not do anything to have everyone in the plant agree to do any one thing. He felt that Saturn had given their employees incentive plans, that include compensation, that move them toward acculturation of specific beliefs and ways of acting.

5. Organizational Acculturation

As discussed earlier, most individuals who enter into a work organization do so with hope, excitement, and a willingness to succeed. To a significant extent, they feel as if opportunity for exploration and growth have been provided to them and they are a blank tablet upon which the organization can write. The organization can quite easily imprint upon them, and if it does not violate any of their previously learned values, they will absorb the culture coming at them and then will be absorbed into it.

Unfortunately, during the past twenty years organizations have changed the above acculturation scenario and have tossed out hundreds of thousands of employees because of perceived economic necessity. As this trend has continued, employees who enter new organizations do so with very little enthusiasm and they do not particularly want to be acculturated. They feel that if business organizations treat people as they have, they will make their meaning come from their family, their network of friends, and their religious affiliations. Such a phenomenon is creating a highly mobile group of researchers, scientists, consultants, and managers who are the best in their field, but who have no allegiance to any employer, foundation, or university.

This phenomenon has had a significant effect upon the way in which individuals wish to work. The structure of most organizations since the advent of scientific management that attempted to chop, slice and dice each job into the smallest pieces to achieve optimal production, is alien to today's workers. Paradoxically, these young, talented workers who do not have loyalty to any particular authority are predisposed to being acculturated into a meaningful work group that maintains the authority and integrity of group action. Ironically, today's emerging organizational structure is that of the tribe, absent any significant signs of status, where all work for the good of the group and take all responsibility that was previously hoarded by management. In fact, research suggests that groups who do organize as equal members of these new tribes, outproduce their brethren within hierarchical organizations by 40%.

Suffice it to say that tomorrow's acculturation of new employees rests upon the degree to which organizations develop structures that will give meaning to individuals within them without the historical dependence upon organizational hierarchies. They will need to be absorbed into small units that are directed toward achievable goals and who satisfy the employees' need for identity and meaning.

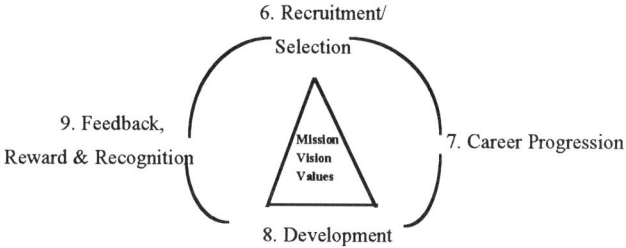

The five items that are discussed below each present a significant challenge to the interventionist. The ways in which organizations evolve each of the systems below significantly impacts the viability of the enterprise and the degree to which individuals within it perform and thrive. The interventionist should be prepared to carry into the engagement the best models available that demonstrate some of the characteristics below; those models should also be in industries and in companies with which the client can empathize.

6. Recruitment

The criteria used for recruitment and selection vary from organization to organization based upon business need. However, any new or mature enterprise should be recruiting and selecting people who will optimize it during both the short and the long terms. Most organizations are still relatively slip-shod in how they bring people in and what people they induct. Those who were generous in bringing friends and relatives of employees into the organization often suffer twenty years down the road when these individuals feel entitled to their employment, are inflexible and unadaptable, and when some do not have the innate abilities to retrain for current and future demands placed upon them. The net result is that mature organizations can have from 20% to 80% of the enterprise who evolve themselves into make-work jobs that do not add value to the enterprise.

Recruitment of individuals to staff the enterprise should be done in such a way that the following objectives are achieved:

1. To provide individuals who have a demonstrated capacity to lead and facilitate change;

2. To provide individuals who have a demonstrated history of adapting to change and who perform in the top stanine on adaptability inventories;

3. To induct individuals who have demonstrated academically within rigorous academic institutions that they can master new and intellectually challenging materials. There is a high correspondence between intelligence and the ability to adapt to the new;

4. To bring in individuals who have a demonstrated ability at working in groups and teams;

5. To select individuals who bring a new dimension of diversity to the team so that additional facets are brought to any discussion; and

6. To hire individuals who are recognized as being exceptional in their field of expertise and who are willing to explore territories outside of that field.

7. Career Progression

If an organization goes out of its way to recruit and select individuals of the caliber discussed above, it is critical that these individuals have a very systematically designed program through which they progress. As more and more organizations move away from hierarchy, the number of management jobs has decreased significantly. Therefore, organizations are faced with being creative to provide each and every one of their employees who is professionally qualified to move, train, explore, and become more productive.

For example, Monsanto in St. Louis designed a development program for the young engineers whom they brought into the organization; they avoided the all too common tracking whereby the only way engineers can increase their income significantly is by becoming a member of management. Monsanto offered all qualified grade 23 engineers the opportunity to facilitate a program of troubleshooting skills development for their employees. These engineers were also on call to troubleshoot any of the myriad problems that manifest themselves in the processing of chemicals. Whereas most Grade 23 engineers could aspire to making a Grade 25 level after two years, the engineers who were forced to stretch by facilitation and troubleshooting became Grade 27 after their two year stints. Monsanto, Motorola, Saturn, General Electric, and other cutting edge companies provide opportunities and mentorship for their folks to grow rapidly in a short period of time. They swear by the returns on their investments.

8. Development

Closely related to the concept of career paths, development is the identification and provision of appropriate development opportunities for employees. At a very practical level, those employees who are challenged and feel that they are growing professionally are significantly less likely to be destructive in their relationships with others than those who feel that they are trapped. To keep employees from moving from *eros* drives to those of *thanatos* as they obtain tenure in their jobs, it is critical to institutionalize development activities within the environment. An example of a company that does an extraordinary job at that is Saturn that pays its employees for knowledge gained, not for seniority.

Not only must enterprises become learning organizations with people in them constantly developing, the quality of the learning opportunities for them needs to be evaluated carefully and objectively. The United States leads the world in its production of competency based instruction--instruction that objectively and fairly evaluates where the learner was prior to training and where they were at the end of training. CBI places a focus upon developing exceptional instruction that most often is trainee, rather than instructor, driven. The instructor's skills are used in the design of the training, not in its administration. Unfortunately, for a panoply of reasons, our country's expertise in this area has not been exploited by organizations.

9. Feedback Mechanisms

During the past fifteen years, there have been significant developments in the ways that feedback systems are modeled and how they reflect the changing structures of organizations. Rather than following the old, hierarchical model of a boss providing feedback to an underling, 360 Degree Feedback systems allow for ten to fifteen people at all levels within the organization to evaluate employees. The new designs provide input by the individuals who work with an employee the most and they reinforce the concept of team. Who would be better able to provide the feedback?

The area where the new 360 systems fail is in how they convert the results to systemic, modified behavior on the part of the employee. Back-ends need to be developed for each of these systems so that the employee is given a comprehensive development plan with the corresponding organizational resources to execute it.

10. Non-Compensation Drivers

Depending upon how distant an individual is generationally from the Depression, as a rule there is a high correlation with their not being driven primarily by money. Demographically, there appear to be trends towards people not moving as they have for twenty years, ending five years ago; it appears that people prefer their social context near family and friends to a higher salary in one of many big cities. These phenomenon cause significant problems when judged by the Board Members who become uncomprehending when presented with these facts.

Non-compensation rewards are those that are designed by the people who work within an environment and who choose them with the realization that they will forego other forms of compensation because of them. What is critical is that the employees be given the facts relative to needed profitability, available compensation pools, etc., so that they can make choices for themselves. They might choose the following as alternative forms of compensation:

Flex time
Additional vacation time
Work unit reconfiguration
Job rotation
Four star crewing
Tele-commuting

Chapter 5

Synthesis

The world that we were born into is no more. Ozzie and Harriet, Beaver, Eddie Haskell, Dr. and Mrs. Alex Stone are gone. Currently, it is hard to determine if such simple folks represented a simple culture or if simplicity was something that would sell in a very complex period of time so that these characters were extracted and served up as something reflective of reality.

Today, we are called upon to make our livings intervening in cultural complexity. We attempt to introduce change into cultures. Though they are well meaning, they do not want change. People do not really want to throw off the cultures that have nurtured them and formed them. It is at this point that it is necessary for us to reach into our bag of infrastructural, cultural, and psychological tools to assist them in moving towards a goal that they believe in partially.

The tools can be used carefully or recklessly. There can be accidents or they can be used like a surgeon's tools. In short, the intervention is what we make it based upon our execution of our analytical and facilitation tools. Perhaps, there is another piece missing. Change intervention cannot be looked at as just another business, like selling cars, boats, real estate or carrots. It is spiritual in the sense that the tools are used to free the human spirit to be all that it can be. To do that, we stop our clients from not listening to the stories that stop their self-actualization. We restructure components of culture to help it move and thrive. We redesign infrastructural systems that have inhibited people from being all that they could be.

Metaphors do not easily come to mind when describing our work. It is a field so new that we don't even have the critical mass to be attacked by the media. Perhaps the best metaphor we can use is Cassandra with a twist.

Cassandra was a prophetess in Ancient Greek Drama who always could see the future. However, she also had been given a curse so that no one would ever listen to her. Let us suggest that the change interventionist must be like Cassandra, as far as seeing beneath what appears to be to what is and, as if working the curse off by magic, our clients listen to us, take our messages, learn our tools, and continue down the path upon which we directed them, without needing us.

Appendix

Overview of the Hall-Trager System for the Analysis of Culture

The discussion of the Hall-Trager system for the analysis of culture will be divided into two segments: "Assumptions Relating to Culture" and "A Map of Culture." Though the Hall-Trager system is extremely complex, it is hoped that it will provide the facilitator with a base for the extraction and ordering of cultural data contained within organizations in which they will work.

Assumptions Relating to Culture

1. Culture is communication and communication is culture.
2. Culture is not one thing, but many. There is no one basic unit or elemental particle, no single isolate for all culture. There are at least ten bases for culture, all deeply rooted in the biological past, that satisfy the rigid criteria by using a linguistic model for culture.
3. The study of institutions and their structure and the study of the individual and his psychological makeup are excluded from the specific study of culture as it is used here, although they are involved in it on a higher organizational level.
4. Man operates on three different levels: the formal, the informal, and technical. Each is present in any situation, but one will dominate at any given instant in time. The shifts from level to level are rapid, and the study of these shifts is the study of the process of change.
5. Culture is concerned more with messages that it is with networks and control systems. The message has three

components: sets, isolates, and patterns. Sets are perceived and constitute the point of entry into any cultural study. They are limited in number only by the patterned combinations of isolates that go to make them up. Isolates are abstracted from sets by a process of comparing sets on the level of differential meaning.

Controlled experiments are set up and the subject is asked if he differentiates between event A and events B, C, D, X, Y, and so on, until all the distinctions he makes have been isolated. Isolates are limited in number. Patterns emerge and are understood as a result of the mastery of sets and isolates in a meaningful context. Patterns are also limited in number.

6. There is a principle of indeterminacy in culture. Isolates turn into sets when they are studied in detail and are therefore abstractions. The more precise the observer is on one level, the less precise he will be on any other. Only on level can be studied with precision at any one time.

7. There is also a principle of relativity in culture, just as there is in physics and mathematics. Experience is something man projects on the outside world as he gains it in its culturally determined form. Man alters experience by living. There is no experience independent of culture against which culture can be measured.

8. Cultural indeterminacy and cultural relativity are not easy concepts for the layman to grasp. They mean   more   than what is good by one set of standards may be bad by some other. They mean that in every instance the formulae must be worked out that will enable scientists to equate event A2 in culture A1 with B2 in culture B1. A proper cultural analysis has to begin with a micro-cultural analysis on the isolate level once the sets have been perceived (Hall, 1973, 191-92)

All quotes prior to the case studies are from *The Silent Language.*

Elaboration upon each of the above assumptions follows.

Assumption 1

1. "Culture is communication and communication is culture" (Hall, 191). Hall believes that culture is the totality of human to human and human to environmental phenomena. For

instance, there is no culture present in an empty forest. There is culture present when one human enters that forest because she perceives the forest in the manner unconsciously molded by her culture. Culture is communication; communication is culture.

> . . . Culture is not one thing but a complex series of activities interrelated in many ways, activities with origins deeply buried in a past when there were no cultures and no men (Hall, 58). Hall continues: Culture is saturated with both emotion and intelligence. Many things that man does are not even experienced, for they are accomplished out-of-awareness. But a great part of human activity is either the direct result of conscious thought or suffused with emotion and feeling (Hall, 59)

Assumption 2

> Culture is not one thing, but many. There is no one basic unit or elemental particle, no single isolate for all culture. There are at least ten bases for culture, all deeply rooted in the biological past, that satisfy the rigid criteria by using a linguistic model for culture (Hall, 191).

Hall dissects culture into ten Primary Message Systems (PMS). Once each of the ten systems have been analyzed for a given culture, the regrouping of all the systems results in the definition of "a culture."

In describing how the PMS were arrived at, Hall indicates the operational criteria that had to be met before a system could become a cultural system. Each of the systems had to have been:

> A. Rooted in a biological activity widely shared with other advanced living forms. It was essential that there were no breaks with the past. B. Capable of analysis in its own terms without reference to the other systems and so organized that it contained isolated components that could be built up into more complex units, and paradoxically--C. So constituted that it reflected all the rest of culture and was reflected in the rest of culture (Hall, 38)

The Hall-Trager Primary Message Systems are: (1) Interaction, (2) Association, (3) Subsistence, (4) Bisexuality, (5) Territoriality, (6) Temporality, (7) Learning, (8) Play, (9) Defense, and (10) Exploitation (use of materials). The characteristics of each of the PMS will be discussed after completion of the elaboration upon the Assumptions Relating to Culture.

According to the Hall-Trager formula, just as an orange is a whole because of the coupling of the individual sections, a culture is composed of its individual systems. Only the first PMS involves language. All of the other PMS are non-linguistic forms of the communication process.

Assumption 3

> The study of institutions and their structure and the study of the individual and his psychological makeup are excluded from the specific study of culture as it is used here, although they are involved in it on a higher organizational level (Hall, 191).

The study of culture in the Hall-Trager tradition is primarily concerned with the study of man as a participant in each PMS and all PMS simultaneously. For instance, the institution and its structure is, or could be, an outgrowth of the entanglement of all PMS, but more appropriately is analyzable upon a higher organizational level. In a similar fashion, the individual and his psychological makeup are analyzable at a higher organizational level, but are not within the domain that the study of culture attempts to analyze. The institution and the individual are elaborations of culture, rather than being culture in its basic form. They appropriately de-emphasized so that systematic analysis may be focused upon a central phenomenon.

Assumption 4

> Man operates on three different levels: the formal, the informal, and technical. Each is present in any situation, but one will dominate at any given instant in time. The shifts from

level to level are rapid, and the study of these shifts is the study of the process of change (Hall, 191).

Hall discusses the phenomenon of how events traditionally have been analyzed in a bipolar fashion. As representative of bipolar analysis he cites: Freud's distinguishing between the conscious and the unconscious, Sullivan's distinguishing between in-awareness and out-of-awareness, and anthropologist's differentiation between "implicit" and "explicit" that were applied to the assumptions underlying behavior as well as to the patterns controlling it. Bipolar analysis then spread to other fields such as scientific management and political science. Both disciplines utilized the terms "formal" and "informal" when describing behavior patterns, management procedures, and the structure of the organization. Bipolar analysis provided a methodology for making distinctions that had not been made before. Hall maintains that bipolar analysis is consistent with the American propensity for seeing things as opposites--black and white.

Admitting that a departure from bipolar analysis may create difficulty for Americans in embracing an approach, Hall proposes a theory that employs three categories rather than two. Hall proposes a three-level theory composed of the formal, informal and technical levels. The terms that are familiar ones have been expanded as to their meaning by Hall and Trager. The Hall-Trager tripartite theory evolved as a result of their lengthy observations of how Americans talk about and handle time. Through the study of how Americans handle time,   Hall and Trager created a "time model" applicable to all cultures. They discovered that there were three kinds of time:

formal time--that system that everyone knows about and takes for granted and which is well worked into daily life, e.g., "the time our family eats dinner."

informal time--that system that has to do with situational or imprecise references like "a while," "later," "in a minute," and so on.

technical time--that system that is entirely different and is used by scientists and technicians and is often unfamiliar to the non-specialist, e.g., "one hundred light years from the earth," as used by astronomers (Hall, 60-96).

After observing how these time systems are used and learned, Hall and Trager realized that man utilizes the tripartite system of formal, informal, and technical in other aspects of life as well. It is important to note that while one of the levels or systems of time dominated in any situation, all three are present simultaneously.

Assumption 5

> Culture is concerned more with messages that it is with networks and control systems. The message has three components: sets, isolates, and patterns. Sets are perceived and constitute the point of entry into any cultural study. They are limited in number only by the patterned combinations of isolates that go to make them up. Isolates are abstracted from sets by a process of comparing sets on the level of differential meaning. Controlled experiments are set up and the subject is asked if he differentiates between event A and events B, C, D, X, Y, and so on, until all the distinctions he makes have been isolated. Isolates are limited in number. Patterns emerge and are understood as a result of the mastery of sets and isolates in a meaningful context. Patterns are also limited in number (Hall, 191-92)

Hall introduces the concept of sets, isolates and patterns in a discussion of the communication process:

> This process inevitably seems to proceed in one direction--toward symbolism. It must be remembered that when people talk they are using arbitrary vocal symbols to describe something that has happened or might have happened and that there is no necessary connection between these symbolizations and what occurred. Talking is a highly selective process because of the way in which culture works. No culture has devised a means for talking without highlighting some things at the expense of some other things. It follows that writing is a symbolization of a symbolization (Hall, 97-98).

Hall compares any communication system to a telephone system:

> Like a telephone system, any communication system has three aspects: its over-all structure, comparable to the telephone network; its components, comparable to switch-boards, wire, and telephones; and the message itself, which is carried by the network. Similarly, messages can be broken down into three components: sets (like words), isolates (like sounds), and patterns (like grammar or syntax). A breakdown of messages into these components, sets, isolates, and patterns is basic to understanding culture as communication (Hall, 100).

Hall and Trager's terminology applies to all forms of communication, including language.

> The sets (words) are what you perceive first, the isolates (sounds) are the components that make up the sets, while the patterns (syntax) are the way in which sets are strung together in order to give them meaning (Hall, 102).

The importance of the set, isolate, and pattern in the understanding of all communication processes warrants further explanation relative to the unique characteristics of each.

The Set

Hall define a set as:

> . . . A group of two or more constituent components that is perceived as being set apart from other things. Material objects such as chairs, tables, desks, and myriad other assemblages of things can be considered sets. . . Sets are seldom perceived in isolation. Normally they appear in context and as one of many in a series of similar or related events (Hall, 105).

Hall continues:

To return to sets, the principal point to remember is that they are the first thing to be observed, their number is unlimited, and the interpretation of their significance depends upon a knowledge of the patterns in which they are used (Hall, 107).

The difference between the set of a consultant's last name contained within the context of Medellin, Colombia and a Denver, Colorado is a case in point. When our consultant is introduced to another in Denver, they are evaluated upon their education, the prestige of the firm in their area of consulting, their appearance and upon their apparent skill as extracted from the behavior in the situation. In Medellin, literally a village of one and a half million people even after the ravages of the drug trade on the City, the consultant is perceived relative to their last name(s), i.e., where they fit into the extremely complex familial structures of the city and, correspondingly, if they are acceptable because of their familial position.

In the western part of the United States, a person's last name has relatively little to do with their potential for upward social mobility; for instance, business successes easily could result in that individual's ascendancy into the upper classes. In Medellin, the contrary is true. Unless a person is a member of a particular family, their chances for upward mobility and acceptance into the upper-class are remote. The person can have all the money and success imaginable, but they will fall into either the *mafioso* or *nouveau riche* class. Their chances for high government offices or for a seat on a an industry's board of directors are remote indeed.

As indicated by Hall, the set's--in the above case, a consultant's name--significance rests relative to its context within a pattern.

In summary, we might point out that the only meaning which can be assigned to sets as sets is what we can call *demonstrational* meaning: This is a "dog"; that is a "man"; there goes an "airplane."

By themselves, sets are neutral. In patterns, on the other hand, sets take on all sorts of more complex meaning (Hall, 112).

The Isolate

If the set is that aspect of existence that is most readily perceivable by man and the pattern is the organizational plan that gives it meaning, the isolate is an illusive abstraction, almost a phantom. It is the element that goes to make up a set, yet, paradoxically, the moment one begins to examine the set closely for its isolates the distinctions between sets and isolates dissolves. To be sure, the isolates will reveal themselves, but when they are clearly perceived, they are seen to be sets on their own level. This transition from set to isolate to set is of great importance. It has caused innumerable problems for the scientist, because when the transition occurs the whole perceptual structure changes. Even the old sets become something different. For example, a set that we call a "word" is perceived. Yet, when it is broken down into its component sounds which are the isolates, we find that the word as it was thought of originally has been lost forever (Hall, 113).

The objective of the facilitators of organizational change is to discover the patterns of the isolates that exist in the sensory apparatus, the minds and the muscles of the client culture. They are concerned with what makes it possible for people to understand each other. They are concerned with what makes it possible for people to understand each other and why miscommunications occur. They are concerned with the structural points around which behavior clusters and which are recognized as being related or thought to be the same. They are concerned with those things that enable all the normal participants within an organizational culture to distinguish between Event A and Event B, i.e., anything in a culture that has meaning for its members.

To summarize our discussion of isolates: It is quite clear that since they are, by definition, abstractions, isolates are difficult to describe. The concept of the isolate or the building block, however, seems to be an integral part of human communication on every level. Moreover, isolates are something man is constantly trying to discover and analyze whether he does it consciously or not. The term isolate is also one which is used for convenience to denote the type of constituent event which goes to make up other events and is as much a designation of an analytic level as anything else. Despite their tendency to merge with one another, isolates and sets are firmly different in a good many respects. Isolates are limited in number, whereas sets are limited only by the possible patterned combinations of isolates. They are bound in a system and become sets only when they are taken out of that system. Sets, on the other hand, can be handled and perceived out of the system but *derive their meaning* from the context in which they occur. Unlike the set which is clearly perceived, the isolate is an abstraction for events that cluster about a norm recognized by the members of a given culture. The actual difference between two isolates that are closet to each other in the world of measurements may be less than the range of variation within the norm of each; it is the *pattern* in which they occur that enables man to distinguish between them (Hall, 117).

Hall continues:

> The isolate provides the transition from the set to the pattern *and is the principal means of differentiating between patterns.* This isolate, so hard to get at and to define, is now discovered to be the key to a great deal of the analysis of communication because it functions on three levels in three different ways: on the set level as a component part (c-a-k-e--cake); on the isolate level as a set (*each sound* is built up of parts) which the phonetician analyzes; on the pattern level as the differentiator of patterns (Hall, 118).

The Pattern

'Patterns are those implicit cultural rules by means of which sets are arranged so that they take on meaning (Hall, 119)." One of Hall's radical, but well documented, formulations addresses the question of what experience is. He maintains that there is no such thing as experience in the abstract, as a mode separate and distinct from culture. He states that:

> Culture is neither derived from experience nor held up to the mirror of experience. Moreover, it cannot be tested

against some mystical thing thought of as experience. *Experience is something man projects upon the outside world as he gains it in its culturally determined form* (Hall, 119)

Hall continues:

> There is a growing accumulation of evidence to indicate that man has no direct contact with experience per se but that there is an intervening set of patterns which channel his senses and his thoughts, causing him to react one way when someone else with different underlying patterns will react as his experience dictates (Hall, 121-22)

Hall expands his definition of the pattern to read: "A pattern is a meaningful arrangement of sets shared by a group"(Hall, 125). He indicates that the most crucial point in the analysis of a pattern is that it is *seen* on its *own* level and without leaving *that* level.

Hall offers three rules governing the formation of patterns: Order, Selection, and Congruence.

Order

> The laws of order are those regularities governing changes in meaning when order is altered. "The cat caught the mouse' means something obviously different from ' the mouse caught the cat." . . . Order has great importance in other cultural systems besides language: order of birth, order of arrival, order in line to get tickets. . . . Order permeates almost every activity in a culture like our own (Hall, 132-33).

Selection

> Selection controls the combination of sets that can be used together. We say *a* boy and *an* arm. Struck and stricken illustrate another case in which the rule of selection is seen to function. We say that he was "awe-struck" but also that he was "stricken dumb." We may be struck by a car, but we are always stricken with grief. There is no inherent logic to selection (Hall, 134). Hall continues: Selection plays a prominent part in the patterns of social relations around the

world in dress, sex, and in work and play--in fact, all of the
primary message systems (Hall, 135).

Congruence

Congruence is more difficult to talk about precisely than
either order or selection. Its subtle dictates may, nevertheless,
be more binding. Unlike order and selection, which have to do
with patterning of sets, the law of congruence can be
expressed as a pattern of patterns. Congruence is what all
writers are trying to achieve in terms of their own style, and
what everyone wants to find as he moves through life. On the
highest level the human reaction to congruence is one of awe
or ecstasy. Complete congruence is rare. One might say that it
exists when an individual makes full use of all the potentials
of a pattern. Lincoln's Gettysburg Address is an example.
Complete lack of congruence occurs when everything is so out
of phase that no member of culture could possibly conceive
himself creating such a mess (Hall, 135-36).

Assumption 6

There is a principle of indeterminacy in culture. Isolates
turn into sets when they are studied in detail and are therefore
abstractions. The more precise the observer is on one level,
the less precise he will be on any other. Only on level can be
studied with precision at any one time (Hall, 192).

Though basic to quantitative research, the principle of
indeterminacy has not been applied consistently and
systematically in the obtaining of data. According to the
principle, you can examine one tree in a forest (set), but you
cannot understand the isolate (a branch of the tree) or the
pattern (the forest). The popular statement, "I can't see the
forest for the trees," is an exemplification of the principle.

Assumption 7

There is also a principle of relativity in culture, just as
there is in physics and mathematics. Experience is something
man projects on the outside world as he gains it in its
culturally determined form. Man alters experience by living.

There is no experience independent of culture against which culture can be measured (Hall, 192).

We cannot say that man has direct contact with experience per se. There are no constants in the experiential world. Each person experiences phenomena in their *individual* manner, which is culturally determined. Analysis at the isolate level, once the sets have been determined, is the only way to arrive at hypotheses relative to cultural difference.

Assumption 8

Cultural indeterminacy and cultural relativity are not easy concepts for the layman to grasp. They mean more than what is good by one set of standards may be bad by some other. They mean that in every instance the formulae must be worked out that will enable scientists to equate event A2 in culture A1 with B2 in culture B1. A proper cultural analysis has to begin with a micro-cultural analysis on the isolate level once the sets have been perceived (Hall, 191-92).

The foregoing cultural assumptions provide the facilitator of cultural change with a systematic guide for the derivation of a general perspective of what culture is and how to map the lines of force within a given environment. Through the utilization of these assumptions, the facilitator is ready to build a picture or map of culture. In essence, the process of cultural understanding is similar to the erection of a sand castle. Once we have individual grains of sand (the micro-units of cultural data derived through the Hall-Trager system), we may then form the castle with the water that binds the individual grains together (the evolved structural patterns of all the micro-units).

The process of culture building is bio-basic or rooted in biological activities. According to the Hall-Trager formula, culture has evolved in the same manner as has man. There is an unbroken continuity between the far past and the present because of the bio-basic relatedness of culture. If we then look at culture as a series of biological activities--activities which are highly elaborated forms of the same types of activities in the animal kingdom (see the discussion of the Primary Message Systems below), it would follow that the facilitator's intervention into that biological evolution is going to have some pretty visceral reactions on the part of those whose evolution is being diverted and modified. Anger, frustration, alienation and failure can all result if the cultural mapping has not defined those areas where the most resistance to cultural change will occur.

There was a time when behavior preceded culture (infra-culture) but was elaborated upon by man into culture as we know it today. For instance, Hall and Trager believe that cultural evolution began when organisms became warm-blooded and were able to react, organism to organism, to the presence of thermal stimulation. They feel that warm-bloodedness provided species differentiation resulting in pair bonding. In their opinion, pair bonding is the most primitive form of social organization that was an important step in cultural evolution. It is important to note, that culture is a process just as is physical evolution--there is no single category for what culture is.

The Primary Message Systems

Keeping in mind that culture is an evolutionary process, each of the Primary Message Systems will be discussed. Through the analysis of Culture A's and Culture B's participation in each and all of the PMS, the investigator is able to construct a map of culture. It must be remembered that each PMS is: (1) bio-basically rooted, (2) capable of being examined by itself, and (3) geared into the overall network of culture.

1. Interaction

Interaction has its basis in the underlying irritability of all living substance. To interact with the environment is to be alive, and to fail to do so is to be dead. Beginning with the basic irritability of the simplest life forms, interaction patterns become more complex as they ascend the philogenetic scale. .

Ultimately everything man does involves interaction with

something else. Interaction lies at the hub of the universe of culture and everything grows from it (Hall, 39).

2. Association

"Association . . . begins when two cells have joined" (Hall, 39). The human body is a complex association of millions of cells, each serving a specific purpose for the life maintenance of the organism. Bodies are, in reality, societies of cells. All living things arrange their lives in some recognizable pattern of association. "Association patterns persist over long periods of time, and if they change at all it is because of very strong pressure from the environment" (Hall, 40). For instance, the associational structure of men changes during a crisis such as war, plague, or famine. New associational modes must be established for the survival of the species during these periods.

3. Subsistence

One of the first things anyone has to know about any living thing is its nutritional requirements; what does it eat and how does it go about getting food in its natural state? Man has elaborated this matter of feeding himself, working, and making a living in the same way he has elaborated the other PMS. Included in the PMS of subsistence is everything from individual food habits to the economy of a country. Not only are people classified and dealt with in terms of diet, but each society has its own characteristic economy (Hall, 41).

4. Bisexuality

Its primary function can best be explained in terms of a need to supply a variety of combinations of genetic background as a means of meeting changes in the environment. Without sex, progeny follow only one line and maintain one set of characteristics (Hall, 42-43).

Different cultures approach bisexuality differently. The social role of men and women varies from culture to culture. Twenty years ago, the woman in the culture of Medellin, Colombia was that of an anchor for family members who, fundamentally, constellated around her; she was the center of the universe of that culture. Today, that structure has changed and the culture is undergoing dysfunctionality until an alternative model evolves.

5. Territoriality

Territoriality is the technical term used by the ethologist to describe the taking possession, use, and defense of a territory on the part of living organisms. Birds have recognizable territories in which they feed and nest; carnivorous animals have areas in which they hunt; bees have places in which they search for honey, and man uses space for all activities in which he engages (Hall, 45).

Territoriality is present in every aspect of life. It is responsible for the speaking distance between conversationalists, the location or placement of furniture in a room, and even the selection of objects in one's "own" space. "To have a territory is to have one of the essential components of life; to lack one is one of the most precarious of all conditions" (Hall, 46).

The office space of a dean of a university usually denotes a higher status than the office space of the instructors in the system.

6. Temporality

Temporality . . . is tied into life in so many way that it is difficult to ignore it. Life is full of cycles and rhythms, some of them related directly to nature--the respiration rate, heartbeat, menstrual cycle, and so on. Such practices as age-grading (dividing society according to rather rigid age groups) combine both time and association. Mealtimes, of course, vary from culture to culture, as do tempos of speech. It should be mentioned that there are students of culture who look at everything as a historical process, and there can be no doubt that if you know the temporal relationships between events you know a tremendous amount.(Hall, 46).

7. *Learning*

Learning is an adaptive mechanism. 'Learning really came into its own as an adaptive mechanism when it could be *extended in time and space by means of language*" (Hall, 47). Symbolic storage is the primary adaptive means whereby man is superior to other organisms.

Learning is tied in with all aspects of life. A child may learn from teachers, parents, toys, pets--in essence the totality of their environment. The child in the school is sometimes required to learn an unfamiliar learning system such as print when they are familiar with television. The child's learning of new systems of learning is laudable, if the teacher recognizes the fact that there are indeed different systems for learning and if they modify their system of teaching accordingly.

8. *Play*

> In the course of evolution, play has been relatively recent and not too well understood addition to living processes. It is well developed in mammals but not so easily recognizable in birds, and its role as an adaptive mechanism is yet to be pinned down. However, one can say that it is interwoven into all of the other PMS. People laugh and tell jokes, and if you can learn the humor of a people and really control it you know that you are also in control of nearly everything else (Hall, 52).

9. *Defense*

For both man and animal, defense is a highly important activity. Man must devise techniques for defense against hostile forces within society, as well as for those in nature. He must also cope with the destructive forces within his own person.

As will all PMS, defense is a culturally learned activity and may vary from culture to culture. Religion, which Hall considers as a defense activity, is much less compartmentalized in the *primitive* than in the industrial man. For instance, the primitive cannot describe their religion because there is not a word that differentiates religion from other cultural activities. Religion is not a specific compartment for life as it tends to be in our culture.

10. Exploitation

In order to exploit the environment, all organisms adapt their bodies to meet specialized environmental conditions. A few examples: the long neck of the giraffe (adapted to high foliage of trees), the teeth of the saber-toothed tier, toes of the tree sloth, hoof of the horse, and man's opposable thumb" (Hall, 56).

Hall continues:

Today man has developed extensions for practically everything he used to do with his body. The evolution of weapons begins with the teeth and the fist and ends with the atom bomb. Clothes and houses are extensions of man's biological temperature-control mechanisms. Furniture takes the place of squatting and sitting on the ground. . . . In fact, all man-made material things can be treated as extensions of what man once did with his body or some specialized part of his body (Hall, 56-57).

PMS Summary

. . . It is important to remember that culture is not one thing but a complex series of activities interrelated in many ways, activities with origins deeply buried in a past when there were no cultures and no men. The development of language and technology, an interrelated pair, made possible the storing of knowledge. It gave man a lever to pry out the secrets of nature. It was the necessary condition for that burst of creativeness that we think of as culture in the highest sense. Well-developed language and technology are somehow closely associated with man in his present form, although just how this came about is not clearly understood. None of this would have been possible if it had not been for the highly evolved infra-cultural systems elaborated by lower organisms. By the time man came along a good deal of evolution basic to culture had taken place in the very systems that are thought of as most characteristically human.

Each PMS is obviously so rich and complex that it can be made the subject of a lifetime's work. It is embarrassing to deal with such broad and inclusive fields in such a summary manner, but to skip over them would be to deprive the reader of a sense of how densely intricate the origins of culture are.

The last generalization that should be made about culture is that it not only has breadth and depth in the historical sense but that it also has other dimensions of equal importance. Culture is saturated with both emotion and intelligence. Many things that man does are not even experienced, for they are accomplished out-of-awareness. But a great part of human activity is either the direct result of conscious thought or suffused with emotion and feeling (Hall, 58-59).

Case Studies: Primary Message Systems

Case 1: Wersuper and Pricey Consultants Inc.

Wersuper and Pricey Consultants Inc. is a Big Seven Consulting Firm that had been doing systems work for Super-Cup USA, the largest manufacturer of Styrofoam cups, plates, and containers in the Continental U.S.. Super-Cup approached a partner at Wersuper to re-design one of their most profitable facilities in downstate Illinois where it had been started up in 1967. The facility had enjoyed large margins for a number of years and was *the* place of employment in the area. The folks there held the strong belief that once you were hired at Crossroads Super-Cup you had a guarantee of lifetime employment.

Delbert Glenn was the Director of Human Resources there at Super-Cup. He had started up the facility back in the 60's and he felt an absolute loyalty to each of the employees. Most of them were hired because they were children of friends, neighbors, or fellow churchgoers of Delbert's. He did not particularly like any of them; he was always being blamed for hiring never-do-wells who were sub-standard performers. He just did what he needed to do.

He never ventured out into the plant that he considered to be too noisy, smelly and the people too obnoxious for his tastes. He pretty much held audience with his direct reports in his front office that overlooked the rolling lawn and parking lot. His assistants pretty much shielded him from any conflict and all of them knew that Human Resources did not support discipline or separation of employees at Super-Cup. Delbert was three years away from retirement and he simply was not interested in making waves prior to his departure; he wanted his final years to be peaceful.

Victor Jackson was appointed the new plant manager at Super-Cup. He came in with a tainted reputation. He had been arrested twice for substance abuse that did not sit well with the community. It was not that folks there were against the use of conscious altering substances--Louie Lou's Bar on Broad Street flourished on every Super-Cup payday--the community felt that dope was primarily for urban, rich folks for which they did not have much affinity. Not only did they not like Victor's personal habits, he had worked in Crossroads before and they just did not like his pushiness. Those who had worked with him before felt that he was always looking out for himself and he did not care about those who worked for him.

Victor wants Wersuper and Pricey to come in and to cut down the manning levels in several areas. He does not trust the judgment of some of the homegrown managers; he feels that they have become so close to their people that they are just like them. They have lost perspective on the central tenets of business. He has made a personal commitment to his boss to cut costs by 10% in each of the next five years that, he feels, will put him in a good position for becoming the corporate vice president of manufacturing operations. In technical terms, Victor is a brilliant manager; he knows Super-Cups processes inside out and no one understands overall operations as he does.

W&P send in two of their best junior consultants--John Weir Wolmott Jr. and Samantha Smith Jones. Both consultants are bright, aggressive, and under thirty. Both dress only in dark blue business suits with high luster, shiny shoes. John wears color coordinated suspenders with his suits; suspenders like John's are not worn too often by the employees or managers at Super-Cup.

The managers uniformly resent John and Samantha from the start of the engagement. They cannot believe that twenty something year olds have anything to teach them. They are especially insulted that they are having to pay five thousand dollars a day for consultants who come over and the first words out of their mouths are: "We would like to do some serious interfacing with you to find out what makes this business tick."

Employees on the floor do not care at all for the two-some who arrive. They suspect them as drug users also. They do not like outsiders in there trying to teach them what they have known for years. They do not appreciate these people looking over their shoulders, snooping into their business and they have heard that when W&P came into a facility 40 miles away 35% of the workers there lost their jobs.

Delbert is meeting with his direct reports about how the *floor* is reacting to this invasion, when his secretary bursts into the meeting in tears and tells him to pick up his phone. He obediently does so, only to learn that 40 employees are holding a union organizing informational meeting down at the local Moose Hall. After hanging up, Delbert goes hysterical; his direct reports have never seen him like he gets. He starts throwing things--his $300 fountain pen, his 4000 man hours without a lost time accident memorial fire extinguisher, even his Lion's Club gold vest decorated with award buttons. All his reports can understand in the tirade is the fact that he has never had this happen to him before and something about: "Punk Jackson ."

Delbert calls a meeting of the "A" List--managers and above. He explains his panic. He and Victor get into an argument and Victor, fundamentally, tells him to wake up and get out of the room. Victor then pounds on the rest of the managers and tells them that he does not have a place of employment in the plant for any manager who resists cooperating with the W&P team. The managers all nod their heads and give him assurances that they are with him.

The W&P Team have a very hard time in doing their work distribution analysis at the plant. No one seems to know anything or just as they start telling them about it someone interrupts them for an emergency and they disappear. John and Samantha have never seen so many emergencies. And it's almost as if all the folks there have premature Alzheimers; they just cannot remember how fast machines run, how fast they should run, what crewing levels are, etc.. Almost all answers, if given, are: "It depends."

Approximately two weeks into the redesign process, Victor's boss in Madison looks at the morning production numbers and hits the ceiling; they are 25% below where they should be. They have been getting worse each day for the past week. When he calls Victor for an explanation, Victor recommends that his boss approve his firing of Delbert Glenn.

The boss decides to send down the Corporate Vice President of Employee Relations to scan the morale climate at the plant. One week later, Delbert is given an award for 35 years of exceptional service and a raise, Victor is assigned permanently to Headquarters in Madison, and W&P's Project is canceled because they allegedly are not meeting the deliverables timetable.

PMS Case 2: 1933 Navajo Trading Post

The trading post had its own tempo. Possibly because of the low light level, most trading posts were pervaded by an atmosphere of quiet, verging on the depressive. Entering for the first time, you were struck by virtually total absence of movement. In American hillbilly country stores, such stillness would have been a reliable cut not to start anything and to be especially carefully about what you said. In the Navajo context,   the message was different. Remaining engaged in their own transactions, Navajo women seldom even turned around when someone entered the post. . . . This lack of response was hard on white newcomers to the reservation, particularly those from the big Eastern cities who bust into a store expecting everyone to reassure them by immediately acknowledging their presence and the validity of their needs. I soon   acquired the habit of opening the door quietly in the Navajo way, squeezing in sideways so as not to let in too much light or disturb the air, and waiting for the proper amount of time for people to get used to my presence. I let the trader--when he was ready--ask me where I had come from. It was in this context, whenever I was working with another culture, that I first acquired the habit of letting others set the tempo as   well   as   the   order   of events. It is the only way to avoid some of the more flagrant errors in inter-cultural relations.

It could take thirty minutes to an hour just to find out whether the road through Blue Canyon from Red Lake to Oraibi was passable or not. Other whites in the car outside seldom understood what was taking so long, and tired of waiting, they would come see what was holding me up. They would open the store door wide, stamp their feet, and raise their voices with a nerve shattering effect.

"Oh, there you are. I wondered what was taking you so long. Say, this place is kind of dark, isn't it?"(Hall, 1994, 145-46).

PMS Case 3: Union Busting Activity

The following scene is seen through the eyes of Jonathan Bailey Draeger, a master at negotiations, who is employed as a national leader of a the logging union. Draeger and an entire logging community have put pressure on the Stamper Family not to make a run down the river with non-union labor cut logs. After the elder Stamper loses his arm in a logging accident, it is hung out to display what the Stampers think about their union friends across the river--the middle finger of the hand is extended.

And somehow lifted especially, Draeger could not help feeling, to him. "To me! Disparaging   me personally for . . . being so mistaken. For . . . " Lifted as a deliberate refutation of all he believed to be true, knew to be true about Man; as a blasphemous effrontery to a faith forged over an anvil of thirty years, a precise and predictable faith hammered out of a quarter-century of experience dealing   with labor and management--a religion almost, a neatly noted-down, red-ribboned package of truths about   men, and Man. Proven! that the fool Man will oppose everything except a Hand Extended; that he will stand up in the face of every hazard except Lonely Time; that for the sake of his poorest and shakiest and screwiest principles he will lay down his life, endure pain, ridicule, and even,   sometimes,   that   most demeaning of American hardships, discomfort, but will relinquish his firmest stand for Love. Draeger had seen this proven. He had watched oak-hard mill bosses come to ridiculous terms rather than have their pimply daughters pilloried at the local junior high, seen die- hard   right-wing labor-hating owners grant another two bits an hour and hospital benefits rather than risk losing the dubious affection of a senile aunt who happened to play canasta with the wife of the brother of a striking employee that the owner didn't even know by sight or name. Love--and all its complicated ramifications, Draeger believed--actually does conquer all; Love--or the Fear of Not Having It, or the Worry about Not Having Enough of It, or the Terror of Losing It--certainly does conquer all. To Draeger this knowledge was a weapon; he had learned it young and for a quarter-century of mild mannered wheeling and easy-going dealing he had used that weapon with enormous   success, conquering a world rendered simple, precise, and predictable by his iron-hammered faith in that weapon's power. And now some illiterate logger with a little gyppo show and not an ally in the world was trying to claim that he was invulnerable to that weapon! (Kesey, 1972, 9-10)

A Selected Bibliography

Carpenter, Edmund. *Eskimo Realities.* New York: Holt, 1973.

_____. *Oh, What a Blow That Phantom Gave Me!* New York: Bantam, 1974.

Carson, Robert C., James N. Butcher, and James C. Coleman. *Abnormal Psychology and Modern Life.* Glenview, IL: Scott, Foresman and Company, 1988.

Freud, Sigmund. *New Introductory Lectures on Psychoanalysis.* Ed. and Trans. James Strachey. New York: Norton, 1965.

Fromm, Erich. *The Sane Society.* New York: Fawcett World Library, 1955.

Hall, Calvin S. and Gardner Lindzey. *Theories of Personality: Second Edition.* New York: John Wiley and Sons, Inc., 1970.

Hall, Edward T.. *Beyond Culture.* Garden City: Anchor, 1981.

_____. *The Silent Language.* Garden City: Anchor, 1973.

_____. *The Dance of Life.* Garden City: Anchor, 1983.

_____. *West of the Thirties.* New York: Doubleday, 1994.

Hillerman, Tony. *People of Darkness*. New York: Harper, 1980.

Kesey, Ken. *Sometimes A Great Notion*. New York: Bantam,
        1972.

_____. *One Flew Over The Cuckoo's Nest*. New York:
        Viking Press, 1972.

Kittrie, Nicholas N.. *The War Against Authority*. Baltimore: The
        Johns Hopkins University Press, 1995.

Kuhn, Thomas S. *The Structure of Scientific Revolutions*.
        Chicago: University of Chicago Press, 1970.

McLuhan, Marshall. *Understanding Media: The Extensions of
        Man*. New York: Mentor, 1964.

Marriott, Alice. *The Ten Grandmothers: Epic of the Kiowas*.
        Norman: University of Oklahoma Press, 1945.

Mead, Margaret and Rhoda Metraux. Eds. *The Study of Culture
        at a Distance*. Chicago: University of Chicago
        Press, 1953.

Mintzberg, Henry. *The Structuring of Organizations*. Englewood
        Cliffs, N.J.: Prentice-Hall, Inc., 1979.

Nadler, David A. and Michael L. Tushman. *Strategic
        Organization Design*. New York: Harper Collins,
        1988.

Ornstein, Robert. *The Psychology of Consciousness*. New York:
        The Viking Press, 1972.

Reichard, Gladys A.. *Navaho Religion: A Study of Symbolism*.
        Princeton: Princeton University Press, 1977.

Waldrop, M. Mitchell. *Complexity.* New York, Simon and
      Schuster, 1992.

Weiner, Jonathan. *The Beak of the Finch.* New York: Vintage
      Books, 1994.

Weisbord, Marvin R.. *Productive Workplaces.* San Francisco:
      Jossey-Bass, 1987.

Whorf, Benjamin Lee. *Language, Thought and Reality: Selected
      Writings of Benjamin Lee Whorf.* Ed. John B.
      Carrol. Cambridge: M.I.T. Press, 1966.

Index

adaptation agents, 64

Allen, Woody, 38, 39

Amish factory workers, 34

analytical thinking, 17

Apple Computer, 83

association, 108, 119

attribution of facilitator competence, 55

balance of the two consciousness modes, 21

Balkans, 57

Beavis and Buttheadist, 12, 15, 16

Beethoven, 18

behavioral maps, 88

benchmarking, 68

Bennes, Elaine, 14

biological reaction to change, 2